D0325878

EUGENIA PRICE

LEAVE YOUR SELF ALONE

EUGENIA PRICE
· 25 ·
YEARS
A
CHRISTIAN
AUTHOR
SILVER ANNIVERSARY

ZONDERVAN
PUBLISHING HOUSE   OF THE ZONDERVAN CORPORATION
GRAND RAPIDS, MICHIGAN 49506

The material from *My Utmost for His Highest* by Oswald Chambers, © 1935 by Dodd, Mead and Co., Inc. is used by permission of Dodd, Mead and Company, Inc., by permission of the Canadian Publishers, McClelland and Stewart, Ltd., Toronto, and by permission of the Oswald Chambers Publications Association Ltd.

LEAVE YOURSELF ALONE

© 1979 by Eugenia Price

Third printing   May 1980

Library of Congress Cataloging in Publication Data

Price, Eugenia.
   Leave yourself alone.

   1.   Christian life—1960-   I.   Title.
BV4501.2.P693   248'.4   79-16461
ISBN 0-310-31430-5

Printed in the United States of America

For Frances Pitts

"Transact business on the grounds of the Redemption and then leave yourself resolutely alone."

Oswald Chambers

Contents

Leave Yourself Alone —

Publisher's Foreword

THE YEAR 1979 marks Eugenia Price's twenty-fifth year as a Christian author. *Leave Yourself Alone* is her twenty-sixth book. She has always been ahead of her time in her thinking and her writing, and her specialty has always been people. Never afraid to speak the truth in love, she continually goes back to the central truths of Scripture and the central figure of her beloved Lord Jesus Christ.

In *Leave Yourself Alone* Eugenia Price has given us another fine book in her own tradition, challenging and encouraging readers wih her quiet faith and her practical, honest Christianity.

Throughout her twenty-five years as a Christian author, Eugenia Price has spoken to the hearts of young and old, writing books which have not only endured, but have transformed countless lives. We are proud of her contribution to literature and are honored to celebrate her silver jubilee with the publication of *Leave Yourself Alone*.

Preface

I RECENTLY RETURNED from the first lecture tour I have made in a long time. My heavy writing schedule simply does not lend itself to public appearances, but this time, for valid reasons, I spoke twice on a college campus and then to a state library association in another city. For hours on end I was in direct contact with people of all ages, and the question which is music to the ears of any writer came again and again: "What is your next book about?"

When I mentioned the title, *Leave Yourself Alone*, there was almost always silence—silence, then smiles or outright laughter. The general consensus was this: "What a relief that will be!"

One lady in her thirties said aloud what I'd thought often during the past few years: "I'm sick to death of examining myself—my 'erroneous zones,' my 'passages'—the works. When will your book be out? It will be like a fresh breeze!"

I hope she's right. For I, too, am weary of the "self" centered books, pamphlets, and articles. Of course we are to know ourselves. There is nothing more pathetic (and often nothing more troublesome for everyone concerned) than the self-deluded person. Still, I firmly believe that only the relatively free and unencumbered mind can acquire knowledge. And because my mind has seemed overburdened, I have turned away from the spate of introspective books which have flooded the market. I read a few of them at first, needing to take stock, as we all do now and then. But as with all products in our Western world, if one sells, the inevitable flood follows. Someone once told a writer friend of mine that she must "go with the wave." In other words, if one book about self-analysis sells, then while the swell is on the "wave," there should be dozens more published. This is known as "market demand." And there is evidence that it works commercially.

Jesus Christ has been called a rebel. Well, in a sense, He was. Certainly He went with no wave. What He brought was new—a new concept of human life. He advocated and lived the caliber of humanity which, if we believe He was God incarnate, is the caliber of humanity God intended in the first place. "If the Son sets you free, you will be free indeed." And the Son went about urging the outward look. In fact, the religious leaders of His day tried to do away with Him because He taught too simply. The learned scribes and Pharisees, the "pillars," spent their lives in much learning, much introspection, much slavish devotion to this and that law which told man how to do this and how to do that and how not to do this and how not to do that. They were overburdened with their much learning and their pride of obedience to that plethora of legalities. They gave full attention to themselves and the extent to which each man was abiding by what had been set down as laws. Oh, to be sure they called them "God's laws," but I don't believe for a minute that they all were. Those man-devised laws were so complex only the "very learned" could even find out about them. It required so much time to encompass all those complexities, to keep check on one's own obedience to every twist and turn in the law, there could have been little time or energy left for merely enjoying God Himself.

Then, along strode Jesus, declaring that men and women were doing almost everything except what God had intended in the beginning. Along came Jesus of Nazareth bearing in His very Person the way *out* of the human dilemma. "You diligently study the Scriptures because you think that by them you possess eternal life . . . yet you refuse to come to *me.*" Now, this does not mean that Jesus was downgrading the Scriptures. After all, He came to fulfill them. But He did come in human flesh: "The Word became flesh and lived for a while among us." God is a Person, not a theory, not a bundle of principles or detailed laws.

Have we stumbled through the "wave" books into a similar habit—the binding habit suffered by those poor, misguided scribes and Pharisees? Oh, we're not talking much about "God's laws," but we are talking and writing far too much about techniques and theories and "laws" concerning *ourselves.*

Now I don't mean to denigrate the "wave" books because many, many persons have been helped by them. I am simply saying that there is deep truth in two old adages which I seem unable to forget. The first one is this: Man suffers from the "paralysis of analysis." The second, and this one is the key to understanding this book: *What gets our attention gets us.*

My recent conversations with those readers met on the tour prove that I am far from alone in my fresh surge of longing to begin again to focus on Jesus' own idea for living more adequately, more abundantly: He urged us to come to Him and then leave our *selves* in His hands. Was He merely being arbitrary when He urged this? Indeed not. The Creator God came to earth in Jesus, as did the Redeemer God, so who knows better how to handle our frustrations? Our failures? Our sorrows? Our neuroses? Our broken relationships? Our joys? Our successes? (Yes, we do, *we do* need Him in order to handle our successes, too.)

The "wave" books encompass almost anything that can work itself into a salable title: books about being happy, about jogging, about Yoga, about cybernetics and biofeedback, about being young, about growing old, about married love and unmarried love, and, of course, about how to lose weight overnight. In each how-to-do-it manual there is a kernel of truth. But isn't the emphasis paralyzing? Isn't the emphasis misplaced? Oh, I need to take better care of my body, get more exercise, do more good deeds, be more successful in my relationships, be more tolerant of the young and inexperienced as well as the old and feeble. Always I need to lose weight, and daily I need to learn how not to grow old stiff in mind or in body—how not to face my future with anxiety and complaints. I need, I need, I need. And so do you. But what about the emphasis in these self-help books? Doesn't such self-absorption lead inevitably to *over self-consciousness*?

Think for a minute about the extremely self-conscious people you know. Aren't they the most difficult to be around? Those who constantly look for slights, who wonder minute by minute what others think of them, who nourish their prickly shyness by dwelling on it and by explaining: "I never know what to say when I'm around people," or "I hate to go out in public because I'm a poor conversationalist." And on and on. Don't you know one or more persons who just must be thanked and thanked when they've given you a gift? Who keep you tiptoing around their personalities because they always make you feel you haven't given them quite enough attention? *Self-conscious?* Totally. Focused entirely on what *they* are doing, what is being done or not being done to *them*. Without a doubt I can say that the most difficult person I know is the most self-conscious, self-concerned person I know. True, she has a minor physical handicap, and it is most understandable that physically handicapped persons might be self-conscious. And yet, one of the easiest persons to be around is one of the most *un*self-conscious persons I know. And his physical handicap is horrible. As a result of having had polio as a child, his body is twisted completely out of shape—hands, face, back, legs, arms—his entire body. Still, he shows nothing but a joyful, thoroughly Christian unconcern for himself.

Being the largest person in a room causes understandable self-consciousness. And yet I was introduced to a group a year or so ago by the biggest woman in the entire banquet room, and she was having more fun than anyone else—totally unconscious of herself.

Well, read the remainder of the book now.

I do not expect to start a "new wave" here, although it would be beneficial for us all. But I do hope that what you are about to read will reawaken your awareness to the fact that the healthy-minded person is the one who is focused not on himself or herself, but on God and other people. Jesus did not come bringing merely a "new wave." He came bearing the *facts* about the only way of life that will work for everyone of any age throughout eternity: The life fixed not on ourselves, but on the living God.

You will find no ego-tickling "wave" book here.

After all, sooner or later waves break against some shore and disappear into the sea.

Leave Your Self Alone: *What Does That Mean?*

IF YOU MISSED seeing the quotation from Oswald Chambers in the front of this book, I repeat it here:

"Transact business on the grounds of the Redemption and then *leave yourself resolutely alone.*"

The italics are mine. I hope that as you read through these pages, they—the italics—will become yours also.

I first read the Chambers passage some thirty years ago soon after my conversion to Jesus Christ. And although neither I nor Kathleen Chambers, who has become my dear friend, can find its source, we both know her father said it. With the passing of every year of my own life as a follower of Jesus Christ, the meaning of what Kathleen's father wrote has deepened for me.

There is only one ground of redemption, and that is

Jesus Christ Himself, who came to earth to let everyone know what God, the Father, is really like. "I and the Father are one," He said. There can be no equivocation about that. On the ground of His redemption, one Sunday afternoon in the year 1949, I transacted business. I turned over the reins of my life to Jesus Christ and for me, at least, that settled that. I have never been one of those persons who wonder about whether or not they are truly Christian, truly "saved," truly "born again"— whatever nomenclature you prefer. I have never even thought much about my salvation as a "happening." It wasn't a happening. It was a personal encounter with Jesus, the Son of God, and the encounter continues daily, hourly as a friendship. Mail from troubled persons who doubt their relationship with God indicates that I've been fortunate to have been quite literal about the fact of Christ. I don't think of my life with Him as a process called salvation. *He is my salvation.* I do not depend upon a process, but upon a Person. The Way is not always easy, but it is always simple. There is no reason in heaven or on earth to doubt Jesus Christ's commitment to me—or to you. He said in plain words that He would be with us always. And that's that. We may turn away from Him by too much busyness, by some willful act on our part, but never, never under any circumstance will He forsake us. Fact. And since He is the Redeemer, we stand once and for all on the solid ground of redemption.

On October 2, 1949, I made a transaction on that ground. A transaction between Jesus Christ and me. On that point, at least, I have left myself alone.

But isn't there more to all this? The first glow of conversion fades, prayer life becomes spasmodic and almost incidental on those busy, chaotic days when daily life is too much for us. We don't stop believing in that initial transaction, but neither do we leave ourselves alone. We toy with ourselves, we analyze ourselves, we dissect our motives and the motives of others, we moil and fret and worry and wake often in the night because we are anxious about this or that.

Where is God in it all?

Right where He always is—beside us, within us, waiting for us to turn our attention to Him and away from our troublesome selves.

For years I spoke and wrote on the necessity of dying to oneself. Not original with me. That's in the Bible too. Jesus said in very plain words that we would never find our lives until we lost them. But as with much of what He and the others who speak in the Bible say to us— we've cluttered the true meaning with metaphysical gobbledegook. We've approached the whole traumatic thought of dying to our precious selves with fear and trepidation, seeing it as a high, dramatic moment to be struggled through or dived into by some means beyond us.

There is an overwhelming probability that the very practicality of what Jesus said about losing our lives— leaving ourselves alone—is just dawning on me. And after thirty years. If so, good. If it has been continuously dawning on me from the age of thirty-three to sixty-three, good also. Just so it dawns. Just so I take hold of the truth of what He said and make use of it—for my sake, for His, and for yours.

There are very few persons to whom I confide my problems—large or small. Perhaps it's my nature to be secretive. I've never noticed much one way or the other.

But people say I am. It helps me enormously though, when I can take time just to pour out a problem to one of three or four persons with whom I carry on regular correspondence. Yet, I find I am doing it less and less. Good? Not necessarily. We need each other. We need friends far more than we need admirers. Then, is it bad that I keep things to myself? No. Neither good nor bad. In the past five years, I have simply begun to observe that more and more I need *not* hash over my troubles. Oh, I'd never make it without the prayers of my beloved friends—some of whom I've never even seen—but they have troubles too. Now, there is a fine line here. Asking friends to pray for us is an integral part of God's gift to us. But the difference between asking for prayer and burdening our friends is a subtle one. I can ask for prayer without going into five pages of explanation. I can ask for prayer without bending someone's ear painfully for an hour. You see, God already knows all the details. The mystery of prayer can become effective just by wordless contact between that person who cares about me and the God who already knows all about everything. Granted, *not* going into all the gory details isn't as much fun at the moment. But it is cleaner.

If you think this is easy for me, think again. I love it when someone recognizes the hard spots in my life. I adore sympathy. All last week I reveled in self-pity, knowing its devastating effects both on me and on those who had to listen or even look at my troubled face. Not long ago, a well-meaning reader who had just met me in a local restaurant said, "Oh, it never occurred to me that *you* have problems." I didn't make that up as an illustration for this page. She said it, and I wanted to hit her.

Getting mired down in real or imagined troubles is not exclusive with anyone.

This is my twenty-sixth book. And if you are one of my readers who thinks I simply sit down and allow truth to roll out, read this: I have never had more inner conflict while writing—even beginning—any of the twenty-five other books!

What you read now is the *sixth time* through this opening chapter. I have left home and fled the telephone and the mail and am writing these lines in a motel room in a nearby city because I was scared at home. Scared at home where working conditions are the best? Yes. Every telephone call began to frighten me. I had begun to feel genuine fear that with another deadline looming and the book unfinished, someone else would be asking me to do something for which I had no heart, no energy, and no nerve.

I moiled. I moiled and sat with my head in my hands for two days here in this comfortable "safe" motel room. Absorbed in the essence of *me*. Poor me!

How many more times can I be expected to turn out the amount of work my responsibilities demand with people on vacation asking, pleading, at times demanding to shake my hand and tell me how much my books mean to them?

How can I be expected to write clearly, to think straight with difficult publisher negotiations dragging on and on and on?

I'm eating too much. Look at the weight I gained on that last promotion tour. But I'm nervous. I'm worried about mother growing restless because she can't lead her usual active life any more. My only brother, Joe, is in the hospital in Nashville.

At least three paid (by me) historians are at work on material for my next novel, and I can't seem to finish this manuscript.

Mail pours in from the St. Simons *Memoir* because it is a very personal book, and every letter lifts my sagging spirit—but every letter, because I am grateful, must be answered.

There is no end!

On top of all that, I'm so tired, I could cry. Even a good night's sleep doesn't help. I am a victim of too much busyness, too many people, too many demands on my time, plain old brain fatigue, and I'm sorry to the marrow of my bones for myself.

I pray and nothing happens.

I try to tell myself that none of this changes God, but the old brain is not cleansed by the knowledge.

What's the matter? The rough draft of this book is finished. I'm in the rewriting process, and *I can't write.* Oh, I fill page after page with words—but they say almost nothing.

I'm caught, maybe hopelessly tangled, in the worst mental and emotional snarl of my entire writing life.

"Well, I'm reading this book now," you say. "How did she come out of her noxious morass of self-concern in time to get it to the publisher?"

I laughed.

About ten this morning, while taking a walk in the sunshine—not refreshing sunshine, but hot, humid, thick, damp, south Georgia sunshine—I began to laugh—*at me.* Up there in that motel room spread over the bed and the cramped, scrunchy desk were pages aimed at convincing *you*, the reader, that in all circumstances we are—once we've transacted busi-

ness on the grounds of the redemption of Jesus Christ—
to leave ourselves resolutely alone! And I was doing anything *but.*

Always, always keep in mind that those of us who dare
to set our thoughts down in books are not super people.
We are too often treated as though we are specialists in
things spiritual. Phooey! Writers are people who struggle as you struggle.

So whether or not you need this book, I did. I do.

I need it even though I'm back on the firm ground of
the redemption, still smiling at my foolish self, ready to
go on with God's and my own business. The little piece
of the Father's business assigned to me for today. This
chapter in this book.

Is laughter enough? Even laughter at one's self? No. I
did not laugh at myself in order to get out of my bind. I
laughed because I suddenly reaffirmed—while striding
past the motel swimming pool—that I had indeed long
ago transacted my business with Jesus Christ. Had I
forgotten about that? No. Of course, I hadn't forgotten.
Then what dragged me—a cheerful, optimistic person
by nature—down into the near depression which clung
to me for days, even weeks?

I dragged me down. I was off guard against myself.
The seventh chapter of Romans waits behind the dam of
our faith to rush over into the eighth chapter of Romans
at the slightest chance. My faith, your faith constitutes
our access to the solid ground of redemption. Nothing

changes the ground that *is* Jesus Christ. But we have to walk out onto that firm ground by the conscious act of our faith. And even faith which is, according to the Scriptures, begun and finished by Christ Himself is in a sure sense at our command. What gets our attention gets ourselves. *What gets our attention gets us.* I did not make that up. But I heard it somewhere long ago, and I still swear by its truth. If God has my attention, then I am free to live up to my highest potential. If I and my normal round of human problems get my attention, I am bound and held—stuck in the mire of self-concern. Immobile. Unable to move to the certainty of redemption. Not that redemption wavers. Jesus finished all that on the Cross by *being Himself* then. That is an accomplished fact. I am the waverer, and I waver for one reason only—I am looking the wrong way. Every conscious step is a step backwards as long as I am staring pathetically in my own direction.

Is looking at God the same as dying to myself?

Yes.

But it is not some far-out theological concept. And it is not accomplished in one fell swoop. Keeping the focus of our attention on God is an hourly practice and has as much to do with the nitty-gritty of daily life, with grief, with failure, with disappointment, with exhaustion, as it has to do with eternal life. Daily life and eternal life are, in fact, one and the same for the follower of Jesus Christ. You and I are going to feel at home in the ongoing life after this one in direct proportion to how accustomed our eyes are already to seeing God in everything. In the good and in the bad. In the joy-filled and in the sorrowful. In laughter and in great weeping. He has us now according to how steadily we've been attending to Him.

"Thou dost keep him in perfect peace, whose mind is stayed on thee."

Does this mean we are to be rehearsing Scripture verses in our minds from morning to night? No. Does it mean we are to go about whispering what we recognize as prayers to the Deity? No. Does it mean we are to speak only of heavenly things? No. It means we are to enjoy to the full all that God has put on earth for us to enjoy—both physical and spiritual—and I see no way for us to enjoy as long as our minds are on ourselves.

Now, someone will surely argue: "But if I don't look after myself, who's going to?" In fact, I've said those very words several times since I've been a Christian, and each time the truth has exploded more brightly: *He is the Good Shepherd. The Good Shepherd looks after His own.* Does this mean we are to be stupid and allow employers or employees or relatives or friends or loan companies to stomp on us? Do we give in to unfair business or personal demands? I see nothing in the Bible which indicates that we are not to use our human intelligence. But we waste an enormous amount of energy, physical and mental, and cause ourselves and others worry and heartache when we turn our attention back to the old familiar realm of self-protection and justify it on the gounds that "if I don't look after myself, who's going to?" Can we keep our attention on God and still handle our business in a way that guarantees our rights as individuals? Of course, we can. But we can also fight too hard, speak too sharply in our own defense, causing our families and our friends to feel sorry for us. By *emotionally* overprotecting ourselves, we turn the beam of our attention so directly on us that we become the center of attention for a whole group of people.

Can you keep your attention on God and still work your way through a trouble spot with your young or middle-aged or elderly husband or wife? Of course you can. Oh, it isn't as much fun, nor does it pad your ego as successfully as if you had "handled" him or her in a way that made you come out smelling like a rose with your friends sympathizing totally with you. But it is possible, and the key lies in refusing—just plain *refusing*—to overprotect yourself and, more than that, turning, even in the midst of an exchange of sharp words (especially there), away from your precious self toward what you already know would be God's highest way out of the problem.

But how do we draw the line?

We don't. The line has already been drawn for us. Our part is to act on what God has already done.

And what He has done is to establish an eternal ground on which we can stand and stand and stand—no matter what. Waiting quietly.

The ground? Christ Himself.

Do you remember the old Gospel song: "On Christ the solid rock I stand; all other ground is sinking sand"?

Not the best poetry—but truth. The solid ground is not a theory. It is not a man-concocted theological premise. It is fact. The fact of Jesus Christ Himself, who said that if we have seen Him, we have seen the Father. If we have glimpsed even a little of what Jesus Himself is like, then we have glimpsed a little of the Father's heart. "I and the Father are one." The one solid ground on which we can stand forever.

This afternoon, since I ended up laughing at myself this morning, I can tell you unequivocally that I stand on that solid ground. Could I have told you that this morning while my attention was still riveted on myself and my human pack of worries and problems? Yes. In all honesty, I could have and undoubtedly would have. And it would have been true, too. True, at least, regarding my ultimate intentions. I have put my faith in the person of Jesus Christ, and there it stays—but. *But.* Was I acting as though my feet were planted on solid ground? On the very ground of the redemption provided by the young Man who died with His arms stretched out toward the whole world in order that we might come to understand the nature of the Father's love? No, I was not acting as though I believed that at all. And yet I did. So do you, even when you are allowing worry to circle you until it hems you helplessly into yourself. *I had not stopped believing in Jesus Christ.* Neither have you just because you may be in the midst of chaos. There is far more steadfastness—even in us, if we know that we are His children—than we dare to think. In God is all steadfastness, all solid ground. Nothing changes. Nothing even wavers. *It is only our attention that wavers.* Only the focus of our attention that changes—from the steadfastness of God Himself to ourselves.

None of my problems has been solved. Outwardly, nothing that was depressing and defeating me this morning has changed. The huge stack of mail will have grown during my absence. House guests are arriving, and as far as I'm concerned, I'm not ready. But God is. And my attention, *by my will*—I do not claim to have received a miracle this morning as I walked—is back on Him and away from me. Although I exhausted myself, He will bring me back to my normal energy. I can count on that because I am off my hands and into His, and He can cope—even with me.

Am I more difficult for God to handle than you? Are you more difficult than I? Who knows this but God? And it is all relative anyway. What is not relative, but absolute, is God's full-time, unceasing, minute-by-minute attention to us. And yet He does not push. He is not in any way a pushy God. Rather, and this may be the key to most of our human dilemma about Him—He woos. He draws. He does not *make* us restless when our attention is away from Him; we *become* restless for the freedom and the peace and the energy we miss by turning inward toward ourselves and our problems. Because of what He's like, we miss Him.

The "wave" now is to focus on ourselves—on our weaknesses, our strengths, our idiosyncrasies, our failures, our successes, our marriage expectations, our friendship and career expectations. Self-enlightenment is good. We need to know ourselves. We need to accept ourselves. But wait. Here comes the key again: What gets our attention (for too long) gets us.

What gets our attention *gets us*.

I have read many of the "wave" books, and I have found some to be helpful, insightful as far as they go. But I tire of them because they keep me focused on *me*. Happily, healthily, after a time I tire of thinking about Eugenia Price. I begin to want some fresh air. Some "native air." The air in the kingdom of God is always fresh, and it is outside air—outside ourselves. *It is* also native to us. Jesus Christ is the door through which anyone can come home—home to what was divinely intended for us in the first place. If we leave ourselves alone—stop picking us to pieces and trying to put us back together again—we will relax and feel at home again in God. That's why following Christ, who said in effect that we *are* to leave ourselves alone, is the healthy, abundant way to live—and, in the final analysis, the easiest.

And so, "Transact business on the ground of the Redemption and then (you can) leave yourself resolutely alone."

Again, what is the ground of redemption?

Jesus Christ Himself.

I do not need to understand all that He did during His earthly ministry or on the cross in order to step out and transact business on the firm ground of the nature of the Man-God Himself. It is not required that I understand. Total understanding would do away with the need for faith, and we would become sharp and brittle. God, through Jesus, entered the human predicament in a way that *we* can make use of daily. He did not become a man so that He would know what it feels like to be us— groping, seeking, weeping, failing, succeeding, indulging, working, resting, fretting. He came so that *we* would *know* once and for all that He knows. God, through Jesus, not only became one of us for our sake, He became our very ground of redemption.

Redemption from sin? Yes, of course. But that is not all. Redemption is so vast, it shrinks the sky of our comprehension. So vast, it dwindles oceans and dwarfs the mountains of all human understanding. Redemption has to do with every area of our lives on this earth. With Him, in Him, we can find a way to make redemptive use of every tragedy, every grief, every failure. Nothing ever, *ever* needs to be wasted in the presence of Jesus Christ. And that presence is the ground of our redemption. He is with us. He is with us in it all. These are themes which have always possessed me as a believer. Those of you who have read other books of mine know that is true. These themes move me through my days—the good days and the bad ones—as He goes on being in my days—the good and the bad. These themes and the very presence of the One who came not only to teach us about the Father, but to *reveal* Him from the ground of redemption. And anyone at any time can stand on this ground.

When I stew and moil and pity and analyze and focus on myself, I find the ground rough. I stumble. I slip and slide. No amount of intellectual whipping on my part, no amount of text-flinging on the part of some other well-meaning person, will help. Not even the minute-by-minute presence of Jesus Christ in the midst of my self-absorption will help if I'm looking inward. I cripple almighty God. I inhibit Him. Fortunately He does not get disgusted and walk away; I have His word that He will never leave me nor forsake me. But unless I am focused on Him—unless my mind is fixed on Him—even the solid ground of redemption does not stop my jitters and fears and anxieties. God is almighty God, but I have a part too, and my part is to leave myself alone and turn my attention directly upon Him. What happens when I do this is beyond explanation. The quieting-down process may come gradually. It may come in a rush—a quiet, but definite rush of peace—as it came to me at the beginning of the sixth time through this chapter. The peace, I think, depends upon our emotional natures.

Our conditioning. Some of us make a leap of faith more easily than others. But we are all equipped to make that leap. And we have God's word for it that when we leap, we will land solidly on the ground of redemption.

Life then gets no easier, but it does become manageable as long as we resolutely leave ourselves alone.

LEAVE YOURSELF ALONE *in the Past and the Future*

THE THEORIES ABOUT "erroneous zones" and the "passages" we all move through and the universal need for "inner healing" of the scars from our past are valid. As long as we continue dragging the past into today's problems, adding all that to the load of dread and anxiety over the future, we're flat on the floor before we know it. The burden is just too heavy. Unavoidably harassed, nervous and depressed, we hamper both our mental and spiritual growth. The mere act of seeing does lighten the load at times, and so the "wave" books do help. If we see that we're victims of either past events or dread of what may come, a bit of the burden lifts.

But seeing is not enough. Putting aside the past and refusing to do battle with the future is never easy. In fact, I view both as impossible unless we know for certain that we are all, in the long run, *God's responsibility*. For years, until I met Jesus Christ, I tried to do battle with the scars from my youth and I tried to work hard enough to insure my future happiness. I failed. We all do. Even after reading the books that instruct us in coping with either the past or the future, we fail in some area. Worse yet, we often fall victim to "paralysis from analysis." Self-knowledge is necessary, but what do we do with our messy selves once we know them? Can we heal our childhood wounds? Can we ensure balance in a risky future?

Can we stand?

Yes. On the sure knowledge that we are known already. The sure knowledge that God is not limited by time—either past or future. His is the eternal present. He encompasses our days—early and late. And we are, because we are branches of the Vine, *His responsibility*. "I am the vine; you are the branches." Where there is life, all branches are firmly attached to the Vine. Our identities lie here. He is the Vine; we are the branches. Vines have roots which grow deep into the earth. The fact that Christians are branches of the eternal Vine is of itself earthy. Practical. Usable. Absolutely essential. This is no high-flown intellectual or mystical concept. It is of the earth as well as of eternity.

Long ago Jesus Himself told us what most of today's self-help books insist upon: We must put aside the past and meet new problems *only as they come.* "Do not worry about tomorrow, for tomorrow will worry about itself. Each day has enough trouble of its own." True. But I find it impossible to follow the teaching of Jesus without Jesus Christ Himself to supply the power. The branch cannot bear any kind of fruit without the Vine.

And—the branch is the responsibility of the Vine.

We can stand on this truth. It is part of the ground of redemption because the Vine is Jesus Christ Himself.

No one is without scars of some sort from the past. The quality of fruit we bear as a branch is directly measurable by what we have done—what we have allowed God to do—with those scars.

My paternal grandmother lived with our family until her death when I was about seventeen or eighteen. I was her pet. She loved my brother, Joe, too, but because he stood up to her periodic fits of temper, he was quite capable of wrongdoing in her eyes. And mother, no matter how hard she tried, almost never scored with Grandmother Price. After all, mother had done the unpardonable thing—she had dared to marry Gram's only son. And in Gram's eyes, no one was good enough for him.

When I was a child, peace reigned in our house according to how much attention Gram received, mainly from my father. My grandfather had spoiled her—to keep the peace—and my father continued the tradition because he was the kind of man who simply could not cope with sadness or trouble or cross words. His goal in life was to see everyone happy.

My father and I were so alike that we both prided ourselves on the fact. And just as to Gram, my father could do no wrong—neither could I.

This business of being Gram's "favorite" made early

scars on my disposition—my character. A pathetically exalted ego in one so young and a nervousness from so much responsibility could have left me emotionally sick today from clinging to this injustice perpetrated upon me as a child—however unintentionally. Only a resolute letting go of my past into the hands of Jesus Christ has healed this. Now and then I recognize an impulse to revert back, but generally I do recognize it in time to curb it.

You see, from as early as I can remember, my beloved dad used me as a peacemaker when Gram blew her top. In one circumstance after another, until I left home at fifteen for the university, my unsuspecting father (unsuspecting of the damage he was inflicting on the young daughter he loved so dearly) kept me in the role of persuasive peacemaker. I never resisted his urgings. I loved him too deeply, too entirely. And I don't remember many failures in my peacemaking efforts.

The goal ever-present in my young mind is still clear to me today—if I could somehow only get Gram calmed down, pacified, back to normal, then my brother could make her laugh again and everything would be happy. In her better times, grandmother loved Joe and affectionately called him all manner of scoundrel; and when he teased her, she would laugh. When Gram laughed, the lights came on for me. That meant no more temper, no more harsh words. But more and more often, peace depended upon me.

Of course, as the years went by, I chewed my nails and tried so hard at everything I did that I grew into a nervous child in spite of my mother's attempts to keep things relaxed and cheerful. In fact, my nail-biting continued until inner-healing began to take place right after my conversion to Christ when I was thirty-three! I have never bitten them since, and through the intervening years I have been freed almost entirely of thinking that I—no one else—*I* can talk anyone into anything. My father used to laugh and say I had a line you could hang your clothes on. He should know! But I *am* attached to the Vine now, and I have direct access to the very power of God to redirect this twisted talent toward creativity.

Once I began to discover my true identity as a child of God, rather than building up resentments toward my father for having sent me as a child to handle what he couldn't manage, I loved him more. There are days now (and he's been gone since 1959) when I think I can't wait to see him again some day. He's an altogether happy, cheerful, good memory. And this came about—more accurately, this began to come about (including my ultimate understanding of the poor, unstable woman who was my grandmother)—in direct proportion to my willingness to leave myself alone where my childhood was concerned. Who has ever had a perfect childhood? If anyone steps forward, I'd be tempted to find a place for him or her under glass in the Smithsonian!

Far worse scars than mine and far less scars than mine haunt the lives of people who have clung to their resentments over those wounds for so long that they now are deluded into feeling permanent victims. The depth of the scar is not what matters. What matters is the power of God in cooperation with our willingness to leave ourselves resolutely alone in it so that we can become whole.

"By his wounds we are healed." This, too, is part of the ground of redemption. Our part is deliberately to turn our attention away from the wounds of the past—toward Christ, the healer. *What gets our attention gets us.*

Leaving ourselves alone where the future is concerned is perhaps even more difficult than relinquishing the past. It's simply human nature to want to know what's up ahead. Fortune-tellers, from palm readers to astrologers, would be out of business instead of flourishing, as they are, if people had no curiosity—natural curiosity—about tomorrow.

At this writing, I have promised another big novel in a year and a half—less than that if possible. Will I make it? Will I be able to clear my head, rest a little, then grasp the details of the vast scope of the history surrounding the woman whose story I'll be writing? Will I be able to do it in time? Then, when I am back at my desk writing—or trying to—what will the first interruption entail? A tragedy? An accident? An unexpected visit—no matter how pleasant—which will be time-consuming? Will mother stay reasonably well? Will I?

The young son of a dear friend is at this writing in trouble—drugs. I try to imagine her fear of the future. The immediate future. What will happen to her son? She has been a loving mother. She still is. Her husband is a devoted father. As with so many families, they are simply caught in a trend of society—a downward trend—one I'm sure neither parent thought could touch one of their children. The future is all fear for these parents. Even though it is a first offense and seemingly minor, he *is* their son. What will tomorrow bring? The day after?

There are also quieter, less showy anxieties over the future among those still considered young. I shared them in my twenties and thirties. To a lesser degree, perhaps, than a bright, successful young lady with whom I talked not long ago because I believe that her generation is far more thoughtful than mine was. Nonetheless, although the anxieties of my age group now are far different, I could still remember and I understood. "I wonder often about the future," she said. "Will I accomplish enough in the years left to me? I'm in my early thirties now. But what mark will I have left on the world by the time I'm sixty-five? Am I doing all I can now to move toward the realization that I have made a contribution to God's kingdom by the time I'm in my sixties?"

At all ages, even younger than the thirties, there is more and more concern about the aging years. Morbid? Not at all. I commend it. In today's economy, one of the most prominent fears for the future among young people is financial: "We're barely making it now. Will there be enough money later on to educate our children?"

I am more pleased than I manage to express that my books are read by people from age twelve to age ninety. One thing I've learned from my mail is that the very young are surprisingly romantic and can still be stirred by a real love story. The word romantic may be a bit uncontemporary, but the need for romance still reigns along with the expectation that God will supply it. I am asked just as often today as I was back in the 1950s, "How can I know for certain that this person is the one God wants me to love?" The need to be sure of a productive life still motivates most people too. "How can I be sure I'm choosing the right career for me? The kind of life work which will fulfill me and still contribute to other people?"

And guidance. "How can I be sure of God's will?"

Well, the one important basic, as I've heard my dear friend, Dr. Anna Mow, say a hundred times, is this: "Establish a relationship with God—a personal relationship—and establish it *for yourself.*"

The young especially must come to see this. It will only confuse and turn us into dry moralists if we try to live our lives on our parents' faith. Faith is personal—for the young and for the not-so-young. And no matter how strong our desires for romantic, high feelings about God, they are not always present. Nor are they always present to guide us into that right marriage or that right career. True relationships with God are not based on feeling. They are based on faith. Young and old, we must learn to go right on when we are not *feeling* love from God. We have to learn that we are *not* going to *feel* loved all the time. We are not even going to *feel* like *loving* all the time. The solid relationship with God is established on that ground of redemption which is the key: We may not feel loved or loving, but we can *stand* on the fact of God's never-diminishing love for us. This and only this prepares us for the days when we *feel* stranded and alone.

And as for choosing careers and mates, God isn't nearly as specific here as we'd like Him to be. There is no trick or technique for "getting guidance" for the future—no matter what our age. But the truth works always. And the truth is that if we have placed our faith in the fact of the redemption of Jesus Christ and have established our personal relationship with Him, we can then *and only then* begin to leave ourselves *alone* where

Leave Yourself Alone 39

the future is concerned. The very nature of God in that relationship nudges us toward right human relationships and productive human work. He always wants for us what will add to us, not deplete us.

Realizing that more years are behind me than I have left up ahead and that many of my friends are of the same vintage or older—what is in the future for us? For me? Will I be bedridden in my old age? Or will I blessedly topple over at the typewriter at age ninety? I never mean to retire. The thought of it literally shocks me. I hate the thought of living on if I could no longer beat this typewriter—or at least dictate words to go on paper. Writing is the focus of my life. So how long will I be able to write books?

Surely you wonder about your future. Surely you ask: "Will I live on and on a helpless vegetable—a burden to my friends, my children, my other relatives?"

"I pray *every day* that I'll die suddenly and easily."

How often we hear someone say that. A natural, normal prayer. And acceptable to God, I'm sure, because He knows our frailties. But how frequently He seems not to answer a prayer like that. I know and you know, if you know Jesus Christ in a personal way, that the end of our days is in His hands. And yet . . . I'd give almost anything if He'd give me a clue, wouldn't you?

It so happens that I don't often pray to die quickly, as much as I'd like to leap into His presence that way. Certainly I have no intention of beginning to ask it every day, because if I did, my mind would be so centered on what might happen to me in the future that today would go by the board. I realize that to some I, at sixty-three, am not yet old enough to wonder. Still, how many of my friends, younger than I, have died! And although He is still watching over me as He promised, "even to old age and gray hairs" (I have them aplenty!), I do wonder about my own last days on earth.

I have never wanted children. Certainly I'd be selfish to begin to want them now so that I could be cared for lovingly in my old age. Will my best friend with whom I share my home die first? Or will I? We will care for each other as long as humanly possible, but what will happen to the one left behind?

My late dear friend, Lorah Plemmons, who died at 102 years of age had, in her last hours, the loving care of both her daughters who left their work in New England to be with her. But they, like me, are single. Who will look after them? Is their present clouded with wondering? Because they live fully in today, no.

Nor is mine. To fear the future is normal. To dread it—if one is old and ill—normal. But to dwell on it? Downright dangerous.

Can we really leave ourselves alone here? Is it possible?

Yes. So long as we have any control over our minds, we can. We make it harder for ourselves, though, if we try to do it from an inactive state. We only become a burden when we begin to do nothing. When we contribute nothing. When we give in to feeling useless. No one on earth who is still conscious is useless. Prayer is the hardest and most creative act there is. Instead of trying the impossible feat of *imagining your old age*— pray for someone else. If you can't keep your mind on the prayer, write it out on a piece of paper. There is no love more healing than the love that reaches out to others.

There are never enough hours in my days for all I want

and need to do. And that's one reason I'm forming the habit of leaving myself alone where my future is concerned *now*.

If you haven't formed that habit, you can still begin. Now that I've written it, I wonder if "habit" is the right word. After all, leaving ourselves alone requires an hourly—sometimes minute-by-minute—act of our will. But I firmly believe that God expects us to begin some kind of preparation for acceptance of whatever comes to us.

One of my dearest friends, Reba Spann, keeps my head above water more than she realizes with her continuously cheerful, encouraging letters to me. We have corresponded for almost twenty years, and I have asked her repeatedly to tell me something about her daily life in the retirement home where she lives. But I still know only that she was pleased that I asked. She has never told me if she has a living relative or anything about her daily life except to ask that I pray that her arthritis pain would diminish a little. Reba is a prime example of a child of God who keeps her attention focused on Him—and off herself.

Dread of the future nourished by our attention upon it can drain us of the vitality we need today. Vitality to work, to help others, to enjoy our friends. Of course, there are those who so dread the future that they run from social event to social event just to avoid being alone. Alone with time to think. I grieve for them. How horrible to avoid experiencing the peace and rejuvenation of silence. Silent time spent alone with God. Not time snatched here and there, but stretches of time outside, or at home with the TV turned off, or at a window just observing what God created. I do not mean prayer time necessarily, although being consciously with Him is certainly a form of prayer. When possible, I legislate into every day at least an hour in the silence—walking alone, just holding a book still unopened—a truly quiet time without the sound of anything to drain or diminish the part of me which must be strong if I am to leave myself alone and focus upon God.

Now, I can hear some of you exclaim: "If she had *my* kind of housework, all my trips in the car to shop or run errands or deliver the children to music and swimming lessons—if she had to cook three meals a day for a family and keep her own house—there wouldn't be all that time for silence!" True. But would you believe I hold to those silences even when I'm on a hectic promotion tour? I admit freely that I've never shared the kind of chaos a young mother's day contains. But have you ever had to make times for silence during a promotion tour when hundreds of people demand your personal attention? When TV studios request arrival at anywhere from 7:00 A.M. to 8:00 A.M. following a sleepless night when a 2:00 A.M. plane arrival got you to a bed at 4:00?

So, okay. We all have trouble legislating times to be alone with God in the twentieth century. Mine is no worse than yours and yours is no worse than mine. Even when I'm at my desk writing a book, deadline pressures and mail to answer often keep me working when I know I *should* be—just appreciating God. Your daily loading and reloading of that washing machine can have the same effect on you. As can the businessperson's round of appointments. But no matter what the circumstances of our lives, we need to be disciplined about those times of silence—whether they run for one minute or one hour. I can always stop when I find myself getting uptight at my desk over a difficult passage or a toppling stack of unanswered mail. You can always stop for at least one minute right there at the kitchen sink or between office appointments. *The length of time is not what matters.* What matters is that we spend the time. Alone, doing nothing except focusing upon God.

This morning before I began to write this chapter, I opened a letter from a woman in her thirties who shared eloquently with me about her one-time fear of the future. She is what she calls a "corporate wife," which makes her one of an enormous company of women. "As a corporate wife," she wrote, "located and then relocated over and over again, God directed me one day to Deuteronomy 32:11: 'As an eagle stirreth up her nest.' And through Mrs. Charles Cowman's *Springs in the Valley,* I came to believe that God did have something better for me each time I greeted Allied Van Lines and was forced to stir up my nest and leave still another group of friends and a home I loved."

This is basic. This woman has caught the rhythm of living in eternity *now.* Even her home is not her refuge. God is. He had been her refuge in the home she had to leave, so why wouldn't He be her refuge in the new place? She has transacted business on the ground of redemption and is learning to leave herself alone, at least where her future is concerned. Obviously, for God to have spoken so directly to her, she had managed to save back some silent time for Him.

Even a little bit of time set aside to remember who we are—but more important, *whose* we are—will help. Time to remember that we are living branches growing out of the Living Vine, Jesus Christ. A brilliant, once-active friend wrote to me yesterday, "You know that I'm no longer well, and now that I'm a widow—shut away on this hilltop without a car—how circumspect my life is, how obscure I feel with no outside fulfillment whatever. No more recognition. No one to talk to who speaks my language. But out of the fire of my suffering, when I use it rightly, has come my first sure knowledge of *who I am.*"

She is a living branch growing from the Living Vine. Grasping that, she can leave herself alone in a life that would defeat most of us.

I am trying to save from the past only that which enriches me today. I am also trying to leave my future where it has actually been from the beginning: in the hands of God.

With all my heart, I hope you're trying too. I guarantee the effort will be one of life's high adventures.

It is all adventure—being in the hands of the living God. Having been there in our past and leaving ourselves there for the future can only give continuity to our lives. Can give the only true continuity.

Leave Your Self Alone When You Pray

THE VERY TITLE for this chapter may sound all wrong. It, of course, does *not* mean that we are to ignore our own needs when we pray. In spite of the fact that God said in the Old Testament that before we asked He would answer, Jesus urged us to bring our needs before the Father constantly. Knowing our minds as He does, it is not surprising that Jesus said this. Somehow I don't think He meant to convey that the Father needs to be begged in order to respond to our needs. Rather, I think He knew that it comforts our human minds to be free to ask as often as we need to ask, and to be specific. Everyone *is* free to ask for forgiveness, to cry out for help in all sorts of problems, but through the years—slowly, almost imperceptibly to me—the Holy Spirit has changed the focus of my prayers.

46

On a day when my head aches, or my back (which is every day), when I'd rather be outside instead of looking out my office window, when in the midst of difficult work the telephone (even with an unlisted number) rings and rings and rings, when the mail brings an abnormal number of speaking requests which I can't accept but which must be answered before I can go on working—I do just plain cry out in my mind to God: "Help me! Help me cope!" Fine. Nothing wrong with that. Plainly I need help. Especially during our nice weather when the Island is crowded with tourists, many of whom almost demand to see me for "just five minutes." I readily confess that those days turn me into a shouter for help from the Father. But I notice that my cry for help of late has been somewhat changed. It may sound the same, but God knows that now, instead of *meaning* "Keep the people away long enough to let me finish the books they claim to like so much," most of the time I mean: "Help me, dear Lord, to stay kind and not to feel hunted and not to feel resentful. Help me to stay grateful that they like my books enough to want to see me at all."

I have not "arrived" on this point. But I am on my way. On my way to learning a little, at least, about how to leave myself alone when I pray. I am learning patience and gratitude instead of my normal irritation and feeling of defeat. Defeat? Yes. I feel a failure, somehow, when at the end (or in the middle!) of a day of hard work I just don't have enough left over to be charming and outgoing. I now see that on the days when the insistence of people defeats me, I am attending first to how they make *me* feel and not to how *they* feel. People who come here are on vacation, are relaxed and in the mood for visiting. I'm never on vacation at home. When I can find a few weeks or days for just loafing, I leave the Island. Remembering this helps me make the effort in prayer to move my attention from my nervous self to the folk who so kindly invite me to lunch. I might tell you that I've made this much progress anyway: I no longer blow my top when someone says, "Well, you have to eat lunch anyway, don't you?"

Yes. I eat lunch. In my old work clothes and in my bare feet in our living room or on the back porch, and it takes about half an hour (if I listen to the news), and I eat about two hundred calories worth. If I accept a luncheon date I have to dress, drive more than ten miles to the nearest restaurant, spend at least an hour and a half at talk-talk, eat too much, and drive home again. By then it is mid-afternoon and I'm through with work for the day. There's no way I can manage to turn the old brain back on again. But of late, when someone says, "Well, you have to eat lunch anyway, don't you?" I laugh. And I've been helped by the laughter. No longer uptight inside over it. No longer feeling sorry for "poor little old work-worn me."

Leaving myself alone in that cry for help at the crisis time eases my way and makes me far more pleasant with the person who has precipitated the small crisis.

Of course, we are to pray for others. And on the face of it, this should preclude any temptation to concentrate on ourselves. I have not always found this to be true. Let me give you another personal example: A friend is ill in the hospital. A close friend. I feel I must drive to Brunswick, across the marshes and salt creeks, to visit that friend every day or at least every other day. Of course, I want him or her to be well, to be free of suffering, to get home again away from the impersonal care of a busy modern hospital. I love the person who is ill or I wouldn't be making the effort to go every day. (I long ago stopped doing "good deeds" dishonestly just so someone would think me a splendid Christian.) But on occasion I have caught myself praying for that person to have a speedy recovery and in my thoughts contending that I need full days at my typewriter without the interruption of that long drive and that long walk because of in-adequate parking once I reach the hospital. I've probably even gone so far as to remind God how busy *I* am and how *I* need that friend back home again. Even when I didn't go that far, I might just as well have done it since He knows every thought of my heart anyway. Real prayer for another person involves leaving ourselves resolutely alone in the situation and concentrating on loving concern toward the other person.

Is this always possible? I doubt it. Certainly it is never easy. There is nothing hard about ripping off a list of names of those we particularly care about. It is fast and simple. But in all honesty, even though we appear to be praying for someone else, we can merely be easing our own consciences before God by repeating the names He already knows. Now, is it necessary that we actually form words about the persons for whom we pray? Indeed not. In fact, I seldom do. At the times when I feel I am truly praying, I am directing my heart, my mind, my will toward the well-being of one person. I am out of the picture for the time required to do that.

I do not claim to be an authority on prayer. The mystery of prayer, the utter breathtaking power and sim-plicity of it, still have me too much in awe to imagine that I understand it at all. I can merely participate, without technique, without knowledge of how the contact is made, fully aware that God has already told us in the Bible that He knows there will be times when we don't know at all how to pray about a certain person or situation. This is extremely important for me. The fact that He knows we're going to get stuck at times is just as important as the fact that He also assures us He will then take over. The actual verse where He gives us all this good news is found in Romans 8:26 and it goes like this: "In the same way, the Spirit helps us in our weakness. We do not know what we ought to pray, but the Spirit himself intercedes for us with groans that words cannot express."

This, to me, does not mean that I will, at those difficult moments, suddenly begin to speak and "groan" in a nonunderstandable language. Some do. I don't. The promise means far more than the actual words of any language. To me it means that when I'm truly up against a barrier, I don't even need words. I need only an intent of heart directed away from myself toward the person through God.

Now and then when someone writes that he or she has been praying for me, I wonder what that person has said to God. What was asked for me that day? Strength for my work load? A much-needed rest time? Was my health mentioned? My peace of mind? The solution to a problem? Or were there no words? Did someone who cares just concentrate on me and by doing so, in contact with the Father, hold me up to Him who knows my needs—all of them—far better than I?

Of course, when we pray with other people—and this is an important experience for us all now and then—we will form words. Unless two are simply met together before God in silence. When my friend, Joyce, prays aloud for me in a special need so that I can hear her, I am greatly quieted and reassured. But for me, much of my own personal prayer life is wordless. Wordless and unstructured and far more "incessant" than ever before because it resembles thinking with God about someone else. And far more natural unless we are prone to like the sound of our own voices. (Jesus also warned us about our "much speaking.")

What *is* God's way for us?

I believe He could not be less concerned about our prayer technique! He urged us to get together in twos or more and talk to Him. He also warned about impressive public phrasing. He urged the closet and not the street corner. But did He mean He preferred that the pastor or priest not pray in public on Sunday at church? Of course not. He urged our getting together in prayer. What He is really after for us, as I see it at this point in my own pilgrimage, is this: When we need to talk to Him in words, we are free to do so. Free to express our grief, our concern, our fear, our disappointment, our heartbreak in whatever words come naturally to *us*. When we are at a loss for words, we can count on His Spirit to communicate our longings for us. He knows when our thoughts are too distraught and jumbled for us to speak coherently. Once we are invaded by the Holy Spirit, His intercession transcends words. His Spirit frees us to be natural. To speak in words or in silence. The strain is gone when we are letting God have His way in our prayer life.

The one thing He is after is that we *pray*. And prayer takes time. But don't we talk for hours with our friends—too often about nothing? Small talk is one of my heaviest trials. I loathe it. And yet even those of us who work at dodging it are guilty of wasting hours in it—with our friends. At one point Jesus told His disciples in no uncertain terms that He no longer called them servants, He called them His *friends*. All He really wants for us is time spent with Him in whatever exchange comes naturally as His friends. He will even lovingly tolerate our small talk.

He wants our attention.

He wants it directed to Him because we love Him, and He wants it directed away from ourselves in the deepest sense because He loves us. We shudder at the ghastly consequences to the human personality when there is too much self-attention. Even the most recent theories in modern psychiatry and psychology now declare that less and less attention must be given the self and its problems. Of course, God has known this all along. He knew about "paralysis from analysis" long before any human mind thought it up. He created us. He and He alone knows what is good for us and what is bad for us. Self-absorption, even in prayer, is destructive. And so, He not only wants us to concentrate on Him because we love Him, but to concentrate on others because He loves them as much as He loves us.

Do we ever need to "agonize in prayer"? Yes, sometimes. But is the phrase accurate? Aren't we really praying *out* our agony? Oh, I know there are Christians —I think of one truly sweet Christian group in particular—who think (or seem to think) that they are not "touching God" unless they agonize, unless their voices sound of anguish, unless tears stream down their faces. I have no way of knowing the inner-beings of these saints. But God does know—as He knows the depth and the breadth of our sincerity when we pray. If "agonizing" helps them believe they are touching God, fine. As I see it, there is no way not to be touching God because God is always touching us.

(I stopped writing after the above paragraph and leaned back in my chair for a minute. God is here. He has been touching me all morning as I worked. And if He touches me, I am automatically touching Him. I also prayed just now, and I found myself saying, "You're here. How wonderful! Now I can go on writing.")

Prayer is contacting God. I agree with that. But it helps me to know that I am never out of contact with Him because He said I wouldn't be. So, to me, prayer is any moment during the day or night, no matter how fleeting, when I allow myself to become *aware* of His Presence in a greater degree than I am aware of my own.

Not always, but often, after prayer—relief comes. And I welcome the feeling when it comes. There are those Christians who use the phrase "praying through" which implies that the sought-for "relief" has come. I think that's fine. But I, for one, would never dare trust my own discernment that far. I might be too likely to feel that if I'd come up with an eloquent or apt-sounding phrase in my petition to God, or felt a sense of emotional elation, I'd "prayed through." Far healthier for me and I would imagine for most of us to leave ourselves alone in the feeling department when we pray. If peace and quiet take over at the end of our talk with God, give thanks. Who doesn't welcome peace and quiet? But much of the time I don't *feel* particularly "spiritual" when I pray. Much of the time I don't *feel* "spiritual"—period. But that's all right too. Feelings change as the weather changes, and I still remember the wise words of the old Quaker saint, Hannah Whitall Smith: Fact comes first.

The *fact* of Christ. Faith comes second. *Faith* in Christ. And *feeling* third. That kind of progression gives me a sense of freedom which causes me to be at home with God when I pray.

At home with Him at all times. To think of Him, to act with Him, as my Friend.

As Jesus thinks of us. His friends.

I have, as have many, been greatly aided by reading certain books on prayer. And yet if my attention gets focused on perfecting a technique, it easily gets diverted from God Himself. Certain prayer techniques free us psychologically, and I do not deplore them. I am merely wary. Just as any technique that opens the way between a human heart and God can be good, can be creative, there is also always the danger that I can become swelled with pride because I've mastered a "technique." More and more I find one thing essential when I pray—to quiet myself and listen and remember that He is my friend and that He is far more concerned with me than I am. In this way only am I able to leave myself alone—in His hands.

Prayer is literally talking things over in confidence—in full confidence—with God. Sometimes the substitution of the word "confidence" for the word "faith" helps. Especially if prayer is a new or untried experience. But what really matters is that He is always there. Whether we "feel" His Presence or not is beside the point. Every minute of every day and night, asleep or awake, *we are in His Presence* and He is listening and attending. We always have God's full attention.

Our part is to give Him ours.

LEAVE YOUR SELF ALONE *in Your Work*

ONE OF MY biggest "small" temptations is to feel sorry for myself—to feel put upon—when there are dishes to wash or any time-consuming household chore to do. Unless I'm charcoaling a steak or making chili or sautéeing chicken livers—and I vow those are the only domestic chores which give me pleasure—I despise anything that smacks of housework. And yet, perverse creature that I am, I love my home. In fact, there is no greater homebody on the face of the earth than I.

My home is a dream come true. A writers' haven, designed and built to accommodate the quirks (they are many) of the two writers who live and work in it. But the house which I love—surrounded by the marshes of Glynn and the St. Simons woods—becomes a horror to me when it springs a leak around the living room bay window or when the septic tank needs cleaning. I love the house but not its upkeep. There are times when I am dead certain that household cosmic attacks are aimed my way. Evil forces plotting somewhere in the universe to bring about time for a complete vacuuming upstairs where I work, exactly on the day when I'd planned to complete twenty difficult pages of a manuscript. And if at the end of another day when I've labored long at my desk at chores that have kept me from writing—the ever-toppling mail stack, bills, and other tasks—I can easily sit in a heap of self-pity over the fact that *anything* has to be done in the kitchen to prepare for dinner.

Now, before I go further, let me make clear that I am not a work shirker. The opposite is true. My friends lecture me to stop working so hard—to take it easy. I understand their concerns, and I try to understand their viewpoints. Many of them are retired and relatively carefree. After all, a lot of people are already taking Social Security at my age. And here I am feeling at the beginning of each new day as though I'm just getting started—signing contracts, making publishing deals—fully expecting to work hard for at least twenty more years and loving it. So, I like to work. Roughly half of what I do at my desk is not done for money. I simply have the usual reasonably successful writer's demands on my time. Favors are asked, and when possible, I comply. If I am forced by my work responsibilities to say no, I am no longer bothered when I'm misunderstood. (That's part of maturity, too.)

Actually, there is one chair in the living room in which I'm happy, but otherwise I'm most at home at my desk. In fact, when Joyce is away, I prepare my meals and bring them right upstairs and eat at my desk. I'd probably be better off physically if I did another kind of work now and then—the years have brought some muscle stiffness—but my *mind* wouldn't be better off. Nor my spirits. *If* I am managing to leave myself alone in all this.

Leaving myself alone is all-important, because a writer—any artist—has the long history of universally accepted "eccentricity" as a backup when he or she wants to throw a fit of so-called "artistic temperament." One author told me: "If they like my books so well, why don't they leave me alone so I can write?" A small, nasty voice inside me shouted, "Amen!" But I didn't say it. And I didn't feel hypocritical for not saying it either. I'd like it if I didn't have to spend so many extra hours on mail—pounding the same typewriter with the same muscles used to write books which people are kind enough to like—but Jesus Christ is, at least some of the time, in control of my life. More than that, He has turned my eyes—my viewpoint—in another direction. I confess to days when I do complain in almost the same words used by the other author. Still, thanks to Him, they are not as frequent as they once were.

What we are attempting to deal with in these pages is our *overall* attitudes of heart and mind where our work is concerned. If most of the time we accept our lot and do our work conscientiously, admitting we are part of the human race and will sometimes grow burdened with what is expected of us, we can forgive ourselves for the occasional blow. Expect it. Some psychiatrists say it's good for us to blow our tops now and then. Doctors have told me that would be a fine way to help control my blood pressure. Well, I've never bought that as a regular remedy. In fact, if I even give way to tears, I feel lousy the next day. My head aches and my eyes hurt. Tears help many people. They don't seem to help me.

Workdays which become irritating and burdensome can be turned into small victories if we dare to practice the art of leaving ourselves alone in them. The key is our attitude toward the work we *dislike*, our attitude toward the busyness. By now you know that my attitude isn't always mature. There are times when I give in to feeling noble, over-worked, sick of carrying my responsibilities—sorry for me. If you don't share those attitudes at times, I doubt that you're telling yourself the truth or that you're free enough to recognize self-pity.

There are sympathetic friends who say to me: "How do you manage so many different kinds of work? I can't understand people trying to see you when they know how busy you are." This comforts me, but also embarrasses me. After all, I am doing the work I love, the work I chose for myself many years ago. I am hooked into the Source of all creativity and wouldn't, if I could, change my days. Changing my attitude *in my days* is what matters. And anyway, I can't—especially when I know of the ways some persons are forced to live their days—be anything but grateful for mine. It's foolish, in a way, to compare my life with yours or yours with the life of anyone else, but before we go further, read this lady's schedule:

6:15   Up, bathe, dress, and prepare breakfast for eight—husband, brother-in-law (who lives with them), and five children.

7:00   Eat breakfast and get the five children off to school.

7:30   Wash dishes and clean kitchen. Do first load of laundry (3 loads a day!). Routine straightening of house.

58

11:00   Begin lunch for husband and brother-in law.
        (Three days a week, she works at the local hos-
        pital. After lunch and all afternoon on the re-
        maining days of the week, she does the grocery
        shopping and the usual household errands,
        plus never-ending household projects. At the
        time she made this schedule for me, she was
        painting woodwork and cabinets.)
5:00   Begin to prepare supper.
6:00   Supper with whole family, then dishes again.
        (Her evenings are usually spent with the chil-
        dren and their homework.)
9:00   She puts the children to bed, giving each her
        undivided attention—separately.
10:00   To bed.

Furthermore, my friend's husband is not "with her" in
their life together. He is abrasive and distant, and, in
turn, she says, she is at times also abrasive and distant.
But the woman is a genuine Christian. "Your premise,"
she writes, "sounds too simplistic. In one way, the answer *is* simple! Leave yourself alone. I know that. But
the route to finding that answer is not. How? How do
you turn your mind off? Especially when others are
harsh and abrasive to you in the midst of all this work?
How do you forget the harsh words and keep on loving?
Too often we react by *not* caring or by *not* loving. Or by
wishing we were someone else, had married someone
else, etc. No good. All of these responses are selfish and
self-centered. So, your premise—leave yourself alone
—is true and simple-sounding. But how? *How?*"

For her, I don't know. I honestly do not know *how* she
should go about freeing herself of the obvious and, oh, so

understandable frustrations of her daily life. The older I get, the less I'm sure I know very much where human behavior is concerned. The less frequently I even try to give an answer. Charles Lamb once wrote: "He who knows and knows that he knows is wise." The converse is true also: He who does *not* know and knows that he does not know is wise.

Then, if I didn't know, why tackle a book as difficult as this one? Answer: Because I do know something about God Himself. In one sense, the books I write are comparable to this woman's five children. Not literally. No book could ever be as important as one child. But my job is to keep myself clear enough and sane enough and cheerful enough to manage an open and alert mind when the time comes that I can sit down and do the actual writing. That is what God has given me to do. If my friend reads this, and I know she will, she will catch the analogy at once. She is a sensitive person, even poetic, and a true believer. She prays. She prays for me. She has sent me verse after verse from the Scriptures, time after time through the years *exactly* when I needed each one. She is kind enough to like my books and to care about me. In all that hectic schedule, she finds time to write to me often—in fact, she does far better in this department than I. But I can't help wondering if she receives the same kind of fulfillment and inner satisfaction from offering her keen sensitivity to the problems in the lives of her husband and five children that she receives (as she claims) in offering it to me. I pray she never withdraws it from me. I value it. We have never seen each other—we may never meet on this earth—but she has sent many light shafts into my dark days. And I fail to see how this is not true with those children—even with that "abrasive," evidently unappreciative husband. And such light shafts freely offered—as she offers them to me—*change things.*

Beyond that, I have no answer. Except—and this is for us all—except God. *What gets our attention gets us!* There it is again. On the days when my overload of work, nagging interruptions, the thought lost forever in the midst of a scene or a chapter cause me to pity myself and rebel at the simplest things required by us all—on those days I am learning to stop dead in my tracks. Just stop it all for one or two or three minutes, or longer if more time is required, and remember that no matter how dull or boring or frustrating life is at the moment, the ground on which I stand *is* holy ground. The living Spirit of the Creator God makes that true. The Spirit which not only lives with me, but in me, makes it true. The ground on which I stand is the ground on which He stands. The very Spirit of God is within me to give me the power to alter my attitudes of heart and mind. He is not in me to do my work for me. He is in me to free me so that I can do it up to my best. Oh, I've heard that certain religious authors declare that the Holy Spirit writes their books. Well, this undoubtedly sounds (to them) as though they're being humble and pious about the whole thing. It strikes me as balderdash. I am the one who sits at this typewriter pounding out page after page no matter how stiff I become from not moving, no matter how much my back hurts or my head aches. But the Spirit of God, through it all, *if* I am leaving my "pathetic self" alone, is empowering me to keep my sense of humor and my perspective and frees the measure of creativity which He has given to me.

We *can* leave ourselves alone in the midst of any kind

of workday because we can be certain that God *never* leaves us alone.

Work can be what we make it—and I pray that doesn't sound glib. God does not want our work to be the same old humdrum for us every day. Outward tasks may remain the same; still He longs to give us—in the midst of—newness, periods of joy. But He needs our attention or we won't recognize these gifts when He holds them out to us. Remember, God said, "Behold, I will do a new thing; now it shall spring forth." But He also added, "*Shall ye not know it?*" We'll miss God's lovely "new things" every time unless we are giving Him, and not ourselves, attention.

In that same promise, He added, "I will even make a way in the wilderness, and rivers in the desert."

The Way runs through the wildernesses of work—any work—and through the deserts too.

LEAVE YOUR SELF ALONE *in Conversation*

IT'S A SAFE assumption that we all know at least one person who talks so incessantly about herself or himself that true conversation is simply not possible. Someone told me quite seriously the other day that in the midst of a long tale spun by a friend on the other end of the wire, she laid down the telephone, answered the door, paid a bill collector, and returned to find her talkative friend hadn't even slowed the pace. Evidently hadn't even noticed that there had been no "hm-hm's" or "for goodness sakes" coming from the listener's end of the wire. "I'd call that friend more often," the woman told me, "if she didn't hold me on the line for an hour or more, or if she'd even give me a chance to say something!"

Of necessity, since I do work at home, I have an unlisted telephone number. But I'm not a recluse, so my friends and business acquaintances have my number. I love my friends and enjoy talking to them. In fact, I make frequent calls myself. I need to know about my close friends—how their days went, how they feel, how a certain problem worked out. Yet, I feel strongly that most telephone conversations can be handled in ten or fifteen minutes. Now and then I confess to feeling hooked when a conversation goes on for half or three-quarters of an hour covering (to me) unnecessary details. There are those among us who simply can't wind anything up!

I manage my impatience, however poorly, by realizing that some people can't stop and that nine times out of ten they are unaware of what they are doing. Another small, but important way in which we can learn to leave ourselves alone—by attempting to see it from the other person's point of view. Of course, if we speak kindly, it is always possible to let the other person know that we have something else which needs to be done when the so-called "sharing" goes on for an interminable time.

Sharing. That's a tricky word. A much-abused word. We are to "share one another's burdens." It isn't always easy for me, but I do share mine now and then, and I welcome it when my friends trust me enough to share with me. But oh my, how easily "sharing" turns into gossip. "I just wanted to share this with you so you could pray more intelligently about it." Too often that remark precedes the telling of a scandal or tragedy in the life of someone else. I don't need to know a single detail in order to "pray intelligently." Nor do you. The reason we don't need to know is that God knows it already. I can pray for you in your need and count on His knowing that need even better than you know it.

None of this implies that we must cultivate the habit of keeping everything inside ourselves. We all need someone with whom to talk. Both Joyce Blackburn and I once had two beloved confidants—one, Lorah Plemmons, whom we didn't even meet until she was in her eighties, and another, our wonderfully understanding houseman, John Wilson. They were our friends—period. Neither gossiped. Neither condemned. Both understood us as human beings. Both listened and always had something to offer in support even if only a quiet knowing smile when we'd finished. Joyce took far more creative advantage of them than I, because of my lifelong tendency to keep my troubles to myself. In fact, I overdo this to the extent that just last week, one of my closest friends laughed when I mentioned casually that I was having some real problems where my work was concerned. She did. She laughed. "You? I don't believe it!" I felt annoyed at first, and then I laughed too. Since I've been a Christian, I am even more tight-lipped where my own problems are concerned because now I have Jesus Christ. The balance here is not easy. We *should* go to Him first, *then* to a friend if we feel ourselves flying apart over something. I'm right in going first to God. I'm wrong when suddenly, out of the blue, I expect some human sympathy if I haven't even mentioned that anything was wrong in my life.

We are dead wrong when we dump it all on a friend repeatedly—*with details*. We are, of course, putting that friend in God's place, saying in effect: "Here is the whole story of what life is doing to me—now say something to make me feel better." With Lorah Plemmons and John Wilson, we didn't need to say much, actually. They knew us. They loved us with acceptance and understanding. There was little reason to wade through the ugly details of anything with either of them. Joyce could meet Johnnie on the back porch when he came to work and say simply, "Genie needs us to pray for her. She's in real pain with her back, but she can't get behind with the manuscript."

Johnnie would flash his beautiful smile and say in his soft, musical voice: "I got a lot of time to pray for her today. I'm going to mow." The smile would widen. "She knows how much we care about her—you and me."

I could call Lorah Plemmons and tell her briefly that Joyce had had trouble sleeping again last night and go straight to my own work for the day knowing that the wise old lady would sit on her own back porch over there in the woods and talk to God about Joyce's need for His strength for that day. Sometimes Lorah would add, "You're both working too hard. Tell Joyce I said to take a long walk outside and look at the buds on the hickories."

Both Lorah Plemmons and Johnnie Wilson are gone now. We haven't begun to learn how to live without them—because with them, we could have *true conversation.* Neither read books, but both understood writers with the understanding of unselfish love. Few realize how much we still miss them, and so we can only pour out our ongoing grief to God. He knows.

My wonderful fiction editor, Tay Hohoff, died a few years ago, and I seldom mention it to anyone outside of Joyce or God—simply because I'd be imposing. I'd be unrealistic to expect most persons to understand how much Tay meant to me. An editor-author relationship is not that generally experienced. People can easily identify and converse about the grief at losing a family member, but few lose editors and housemen and centenarians (Lorah Plemmons was 102 when she died). To attempt to converse about my grief at losing them would simply turn into a one-sided conversation focused on me. Leaving myself alone in the hands of God in the sorrow has been spiritually strengthening.

I'd call one friend more often if I thought there was any chance that she wouldn't keep me on the telephone for an hour talking about her husband who died twelve years ago! She always tells me before she hangs up that it helps her so much to have a conversation with me, and I smile to myself. I haven't managed to say more than a few words. There has been no real conversation.

Another woman revels in giving me plane schedules, full accounts of lost luggage, people met on the plane, etc., etc., etc., ad nauseam every time her son comes home from his job in the west. I love this woman. She has many traits which I deeply admire, and often my hand is on the telephone to call her when I think—no, I just can't face all that again. I tried telling her about my editor's death soon after it happened. "That's too bad," she replied, "but you're so well-established you'll find another good one." And zoom. She was launched into an endless description of her son's latest trip home.

Well, our problem is that we don't often take an objective look at ourselves in these areas. We don't *hear* ourselves. We know what interests us, and we assume it interests everyone else too. Natural? Yes. But thoughtless. It throws us off-center in more than conversation. On earth, Jesus Christ was all balance. This is one of the first things I look for in His followers. Balance. My lack of it, as I said, is going overboard keeping personal problems to myself when I often could be helped by getting another viewpoint. When I could be comforted by an understanding word or look. I keep personal problems inside, and with me, personal problems include trouble with my writing. Then I'm surprised when I get so little sympathy if I do happen to mention a tough day, slogging through a scene. No one suspects that I am not sailing along.

But although I'm improving and I know it, I often did exhaust people by talking about books in general and mine in particular. Not the actual writing—but the stories. Obviously, nothing on earth interests me as much as books. Last night at the dinner table, Joyce and our guest fell into a heated discussion of current women's styles. I sat there with my mind wandering for a while and then began to clear the table. Not very polite of me, but I had nothing to add because clothes have always bored me. And in the kitchen, loading the dishwasher, I remembered a night five or six years ago when Joyce reminded me gently that all evening I had monopolized the conversation talking about research for one of my novels. I stopped scraping plates and slipped back into my place at the table and tried to say a word or two about fashions.

"You're just so excited over books," she had said on that long-ago night, "that you do sometimes talk quite a lot about research, etc. You're not boasting, you're just excited. But tonight, our host got glassy-eyed. I don't think you noticed."

From my heart, I thanked her, and I will say that since that night, I *hear* myself when I begin to entertain myself with book talk! I hear me when I begin to go on at length about my great research helpers in Atlanta, Savannah, Jacksonville, St. Augustine, and how blind alleys often lead to whole areas of new information. How excited I am when research time is at hand because it's like a treasure hunt. Interesting stuff for a while, perhaps. But not for long to someone who hasn't experienced it.

Mental alertness is required in conversation. And ears that hear our own voices as well as the voices around us. And sensitivity to God Himself, who loves those who are forced to listen as much as He loves the talkers.

Dr. Wayne W. Dyer, author of the best seller, *Your Erroneous Zones*, declares rightly that "Virtually all fights revolve around the erroneous thought, 'If you were only more like me, I wouldn't have to be upset.'" He then goes on to urge that we accept others as they are. Excellent. He urges us to realize that we are all different. Of course we are. But accepting this, and acting on it is not easy. Nor does Dyer claim it to be. What I'd like to add here is that for the Christian, while we must also accept others as they are, realizing that no two persons think alike, there is more.

There is the definite potential of active *identification*.

Jesus Christ came to earth to identify with us. I have written this before from other angles; I must say it again because it is the key: He came, not because He needed to know what it felt like to be human—He already knew. "Without him was not any thing made that was made." Christ was there with the Father at Creation. As I see it, He came to earth, limiting Himself as we are limited, so that *we would know that He knows*. And for us in our human relationships, which always include conversation of one sort or another, the big plus is here: the Spirit—the living Spirit of this same Jesus Christ—dwells in each of His followers. Wherever that Spirit is, there is total ability to *identify* no matter how unlike us the other person may be. Didn't Jesus Christ identify with the entire human race? And could there be any two people more unlike than Jesus on his cross and the men who put Him there? During those ghastly hours, He cried out for the Father's forgiveness toward those very men because "they know not what they do." He was so completely identified with His enemies that he experienced their darkness, their lack of understanding of who He really was, their sin. Isn't it true that He took our sin into His own body on that cross? Limited though we are by our human frailties, we as Christians have access—direct access—to His kind of identification.

One of the surest ways to leave ourselves alone—to keep peace in conversation—is to identify with the other person, thereby maintaining our own peace. Identifying is not agreeing with. It is merely being free enough of ourselves to recognize another point of view and to leave some fruitless things left unsaid.

It is thought to be easier to leave oneself alone in a business conversation than in a more personal one. And yet, is it really? If a man is discussing his own future job possibilities with his superior, how objective is he? If a woman is holding her ground with a career superior, requesting a deserved raise or a renewed contract, how objective is she? How about bargaining with a contractor over the cost of a new roof? I don't remember having read much, if anything, in Christian books about such conversations as these. Oh, the secular self-help books offer excellent advice here, on a humanistic premise, but what of the Christian in a conversation of this nature and importance? Is he or she to be overly submissive, a yes-man, a yes-woman? As in any other human exchange, we as Christians are to leave ourselves alone in the area of overt self-defense and emotional tirades. But if we truly believe that our affairs, all of them, are in God's hands, are we to agree to just anything? Anything to keep the job or the contract or the peace? No. It is not that simple.

First of all, we must be realistic in such talks, particularly employment discussions. We must have done our own homework where our individual worth to the business firm or institution is concerned. To stay on safe ground here, I'll use myself and my own publishing negotiations as an example. At regular intervals I check up on my book sales. The personnel at the publishing houses may be fond of me and I of them, but the publishing world does not operate·on friendship. It operates on the margin of profit *to the publisher.* I may get rave letters from readers, but if there haven't been thousands more readers who paid their money for my book, high enthusiasm from a few is only nice, *not* effective when negotiating a new contract.

Cognizant of all these facts and more, which I will not belabor, I approach the conversation concerning a new publishing contract. With all my heart, I try to be realistic about my worth to the company. I try neither to overestimate it nor to underestimate my value as an author. Once this is clear to *me,* my emotions do not enter into much of what will be said between the house representative and me. If I let my financial needs govern the size of the advance I request, now and then I'd be asking for a whopper. This would not be leaving myself alone since no publisher is in the business of being a benefactor. They are all in the business of making a profit. As I am in the business of earning a living by writing the books they publish.

So, armed with the facts—and what has become a habit of schooling myself to *identify* with the publisher's problems as well as my own—we hold conversation. Some measure of identification with my publishers usually makes it possible for these conversations to come off without rancor. We are each obligated to stand by our own principles, and conflicts are inevitable, but conversation—real communication from both sides—is possible. We can stick to our principles without being stuck with unreasonable egos and with the very real freedom of leaving our touchy selves alone in the process.

One of the most troublesome conversational areas for both believer and nonbeliever occurs in the time spent visiting with relatives.

I've lost track of the number of letters I've received from grown-up sons and daughters who find conversation difficult with their parents. Not only difficult, but often boring and quarrelsome. This is far from uncommon. Mother and dad and Aunt Minnie and Uncle John are still in the same familiar surroundings with the same old interests. The children have built new lives of their own, acquired new interests, and find it hard to communicate with the homefolk. If the offspring don't show sufficient interest—trouble. "You don't love us any more." "You've gotten too sophisticated." Or as Grandmother Price might have said, "You're too big for your britches." When the young people try to involve parents and other older relatives in *their* lives, they are often greeted with silence, confusion, or disinterest. "Every time I try to tell mother about my work in the classroom, she listens for about thirty seconds and begins to talk about how much trouble she's having getting her plumbing repaired!"

Well, if parents are quite old, this is understandable. In most of the letters I receive, though, the complaints come from younger marrieds or singles with middle-aged parents. Of course, parents become frustrated too. One-sided conversation can and does occur when the younger members of a family *have* shut out the older relatives.

The solution? Identification on both sides. And it won't always come simultaneously either. That faulty plumbing is as real to mother as school is to daughter. A little understanding of this—even a small amount by at least one person—helps enormously. And most of the time it is less difficult for the younger person to yield a little. No matter how much the teacher would like her mother to be interested in her life at school, leaving herself alone long enough to hear mother out on the plumbing problem *will* help.

Emotions flare and defenses spring up. There are no easy solutions to our conversation handicaps, but the basic premise of this book does enable us to cope. It isn't easy—sometimes it's downright hard—but leaving ourselves alone long enough to hear someone else out can work wonders. There is no one from whom we can't learn something.

LEAVE YOUR SELF ALONE *in Diversity*

I AM A Christian. The Quaker writers would call me a *convinced* believer. I am no less certain now than at the time of my conversion to Christ that He *is* the way. Yet today I am far less dogmatic in the sharing of that conviction. And I'm sure God is relieved that I am. In fact, He brought about my freedom from the dogmatic heart. I see no hint of dogmatism in Christ.

Certainty? Yes.

Dogmatism? No.

I still experience the same kind of joy when I learn that someone has just met Jesus Christ. In fact, my joy runs deeper than it did all those years ago when *I* first met Him. It deepens every day because, for me, the God I worship grows larger, more powerful, more loving, more faithful with the passing of every day. The

75

truth is, of course, that He does not grow in any of these ways—He has always been complete. It is my "sight" of Him that grows, and so to me He is more and more and more. I understand now that because of this, He needs my defense less and less and less. In fact, God needs no defense from anyone. He is God. And so in any discussion of religion, I am freer than I ever thought possible. Freer of myself. Freed from the dogmatic heart by this God I follow. I have no need of dogmatism. *He is my certainty.* Jesus Christ did a finished work on His cross. I don't understand what He did—no one does—but it was finished. His heart has been revealed. If we have learned to "see" God in Jesus Christ and not according to the joys or hardships of our personal lives, not according to dogma, certainty comes.

Jesus is God's explanation for everything.

As a new Christian, I did what almost every convinced new believer does: I argued with and pressured and antagonized those who did not yet see God in Christ. Sad to say, there are still those who go right on doing this after many years as Christians. Unlike many, however, I had dug into the other religions before I gave Christ a chance in my life. In them I found much that was true—much of half-truth, much that inspired and lifted my human spirit. But in Christ I found *forgiveness,* and no other religion offers that. So, for about fifteen years I banged people over the head with that magnificent truth, using it to "prove" that I was right and they were wrong.

Herein lies the key: The slightest hint of such self-righteousness is sin. And it repels. The scribes and the Pharisees argued on this level with Jesus when He was on earth. And why wouldn't they? They argued from their intellects, out of their store of knowledge of the law. Religious law. Jesus did not argue back. He simply stood there in His God-authority and quietly declared: "I am the Way." He made no arguments.

Slowly, with the passing of the years, I have discovered that He still stands—right in the room where we are holding our religious conversation—saying, not just to the person we are trying to convince, but to us too, that He is the Way. Even for those who during His earthly ministry tried to catch Him up on the Scriptures (and the world is still full of text-flingers), He had a quiet, certain answer: "You diligently study the Scriptures because you think that by them you possess eternal life. These are the Scriptures that testify about me, yet you refuse to come to me to have life."

Even then, He was trying to help people see that we are not to worship and "prove" the Scriptures but to *search* the Scriptures in order to find out that He and He alone is the Way!

Let no one misunderstand here; I believe the Holy Bible to be the Word of God. I do not understand all of it (who does?), but I believe it. Yet, it is Jesus Christ whom I follow. On whom I depend. The most glorious fact I know is that He is *not* a theory, not a dogma; He is a Person. A knowable Person—today. There is no way that He cannot be contemporary—He thought up everything! He lived His earthly life bound by time in His humanity, but He was also God and He remained God even as He was being tempted in all things exactly as we are tempted. How is this possible? I don't know. No one but God knows. There *is* the matter of faith that Jesus was (is) God's revelation of Himself. There have always been and will always be swings to and away from belief in the deity of Christ. There was a period in the past when God was declared "dead." It strikes man now and then as being too good to be true that God Himself worked out a way to visit Earth, to become one of us. But then, as my beloved friend, the late E. Stanley Jones, used to say, "It is too good *not* to be true."

If you have read several of my older books (focused in *What Is God Like?*), you will have followed my growing conviction that the deity of Jesus Christ is central to all Christian faith. Year by year, sometimes day by day, I become more convinced that this is true. In any discussion with anyone about my faith, I have no choice but to make that clear. If God had not revealed Himself in a human being with a human heart and lungs and eyes and ears and arms and temptations, I could not have followed Him. I became a believer because of this central fact, and my faith is strengthened because of it. It is still an amazement to me. I can still be overcome by the fact that the young Man hanging on His cross with His arms outstretched toward the whole world—was God Himself. All that could be contained of God in a human being. I have said it a thousand times, I have written it in book after book—I must repeat it here: Christians are not moralists who follow a set of religious principles. Christians are those fortunate folk who have discovered the nature of God in Jesus Christ. The forgiving, living Jesus Christ. The still-living Jesus Christ.

"No man hath seen God at any time; the only begotten Son . . . he hath declared him." He, Jesus, has made the Father known.

It should be clear by now that my own conviction concerning the central issue of Christianity—the deity of Jesus Christ—is firm. When I pray for someone who still does not know Him as He is, that is the way I pray. "Dear Lord, show her—show him—who You are." Freedom opens outward from that point. "If the Son shall make you free, you shall be free indeed."

Jesus said that unless we become as little children we cannot possibly know what the kingdom of God is about. The more childlike I grow about Him, the firmer my own central conviction becomes. So, the fact that I am learning (and succeeding most of the time) to leave myself alone during a religious discussion has nothing to do with my self-control. It has everything to do with my certainty that *the living God can testify to Himself.* Oh, of course, in my writing and in conversation I voice my personal conviction that the Father is knowable in Jesus. That they are, as Jesus said—one. But if someone climbs down my throat for saying it, I can now smile and let it go. There often comes a time when our part is to shut up and begin to pray. Not long ago someone, itching for a religious argument with me, snapped: "You look too peaceful about this whole thing. I don't have any hopes of an argument here!" If I did look peaceful, it had nothing to do with the way in which I'd set my features. It had everything to do with leaving myself alone in order to give the living Lord a chance.

Leaving ourselves alone in a religious discussion does not mean clamming up, refusing to communicate our faith. It means being certain enough of Christ Himself to trust His personal involvement—not only in convincing the other person, but in building our own certainty.

Christians can swing the old egos in arguments with each other too—about baptism, the Bible, eternal security, ordaining women, and so on and on and on. Making secondary, as they talk, the fact that only Jesus Christ is central.

But religious diversity is not the only place where He must be kept central. Jesus Christ must be remembered in all diversity. Oh, perhaps not by name, but in spirit, in attitudes of heart. Jesus did not have a rigid mind. His mind was simply certain with the authority of His Father.

Egos flame over religious differences; they flame even higher at times over politics. Do we need to keep Christ central in our political diversities?

I say, He'd better be there—smack in the center.

I wrote the above and then stopped for lunch. As we often do, Joyce and I talked a little about my upcoming afternoon's work. We agreed that political discussions can be so incendiary because politics as such is amoral. Political loyalties do not spring from one central source as does faith. All my life, until I began to think for myself and become influenced by what I saw around me in our social system, I voted my father's party line. (Both he and mother were registered Republicans.) It is common for children to follow in their parents' political footsteps. I happen to be a Democrat now—a National Democrat, not a reactionary one—by choice. However, if I did not believe in the Democratic presidential candidate and liked the Republican, I could easily vote that way. (None of this is a treatise for or against either party. I am first and foremost independent in my thinking and strongly in support of our two-party system. I am simply using illustrations from the life I know best—my own.)

Jimmy Carter is president as I write this. I believe in him. Not because he is a Georgian, but because I had the chance to watch him as governor of Georgia. I believe in the strength of his Christian faith. His original mind. His caring heart. If anything, he's a bit conservative for my blood, but then he knows a lot more about managing government than I do. I simply trust his judgment.

Now . . . if you dislike and distrust him, do you still love me? I still love you. And sitting quietly while some of my friends take him apart is not easy. Do I sit quietly by, saying nothing? Of course not. I speak my piece as I've done here. *But*, I make every effort (successful sometimes!) to identify with my friends north and south, east and west, who do not like him for any of a number of reasons. Not the least, it seems, is his southern drawl and his seemingly ineffectual speaking style. Neither bothers me. Both would have once. I held a prejudice a mile wide against white southerners until I became one when I fell in love with St. Simons Island, Georgia, back in 1961. I live surrounded by quiet-mannered, *seemingly* unaggressive men like President Carter—my friends at the insurance office, the bank, my attorney. Believe me, they are anything but ineffectual!

Do I always find it easy to discover that, unknown to me, a friend has been on the other side of the political fence? No. Just recently, two of my oldest and dearest friends from the publishing world visited us for a weekend. I sounded off in my positive manner about President Carter, fully expecting them to be of the same political persuasion as are 99 percent of my New York publishing friends. They were *not*, and suddenly silence fell like a blow into my living room. I confess, I did have a brief inward struggle. Then it all struck me as funny. For about thirty seconds, or maybe longer, I did *not* leave myself and my pet political philosophy alone!

Then, thank heaven, I did. We had our best moments of laughter during the remainder of their visit, making jokes in both directions about our differing views.

My brother and I are on opposite sides of the fence where politics is concerned. I'm a strong proponent of federal gun-control laws. He's as hotly against them because he works for Remington, a maker of firearms. But Joe and I love each other, and we can talk for an hour about the issue and come out hugging as energetically as in the old days when we played together under the walnut tree in the backyard. Love—and God is love—makes it possible for us both to leave ourselves alone in disagreement.

Georgia once had a fanatically religious and rather bizarre man as governor (Lester Maddox) who declared that God is a Democrat. I doubt that. I also doubt that God is a Republican. God is God, and He is the eternal weight. When we shift Him to the margin (and I wrote this in my very first book twenty-five years ago), everything tips. The whole works shifts to one side. With Jesus Christ in the center—dead center—we become balanced people. Mature. Able to leave ourselves alone even in political discussions.

I look for balance in estimating the depth of any Christian commitment. Balance and sanity. It has been said that Jesus Christ was all sanctity, but He was also all sanity. I believe it. There is no balance without sanity. There is no ongoing, dependable, uncontroversial love without balance.

You are entitled to your opinions on any number of issues. So am I. But you need to love me if I disagree with you. Because I need your love. I need to love you if you disagree with me because you need my love too.

Gradually, I am discovering the freedom of learning to love in diversity. We are all slow at this. But we can hurry it up a little if we set our selfish, opinionated egos to one side and allow God to move to the center where *He knows* He needs to be if we are to enjoy the peace He said He was leaving us: "Peace I leave with you, my peace I give unto you: not as the world giveth, give I unto you."

Why is it, then, if we have this peace from God Himself, that we are so often antagonistic? The answer is so simple we miss it: Love is essential to peace. There is no peace outside of God, and God is love. That is why in order for us to receive the peace He left us, He and He alone must stand central. Not our precious opinions, but Christ. The writer to the Romans, as J. B. Phillips paraphrases it, encapsules the whole truth: "Don't become snobbish but take a real interest in ordinary people. Don't become set in your own opinions. . . . live at peace with everyone." *Everyone.* Even those who disagree with us. Especially those.

It is possible to learn a little more about the freedom which comes as a direct result of being able to love in diversity. Love remains the answer.

LEAVE YOUR SELF ALONE *in Illness and Grief*

FIRST OF ALL let me make clear that "family" as I use the word is not necessarily limited to one's blood relations. God sets us down in families which often are not hereditary. Which can be even more meaningful because He allowed us to choose the members of these families. A friend, proven true, proven understanding, is far more deeply set in the heart than a selfish, touchy sister or a domineering parent. I happen to have a mother who does understand me, who does care unselfishly about my well-being. The same is true of my brother. But this is not true in every family.

And yet society as a whole seems unwilling or unable to recognize that grief and sorrow over the illness or death of a close friend cuts as harshly as grief and sorrow over the illness or death of an immediate family member. I can testify to this firsthand. I suffered intensely, fought to keep my anxieties under control and to go on writing during the long, dark weeks in which I could feel my beloved editor, Tay Hohoff, slipping away. She was in New York City, I on St. Simons Island, Georgia. In a whisk, I would have hopped a plane, but I loved her too much. In her last desperate, but admirable attempt to hold to that good independence—not to burden anyone (*anyone*) with her problems—she would have resisted my coming. I was frightened at losing her editing expertise where my own work was concerned—but much more than that, I loved her with all my heart as a human being. When she died, I felt bereft. Left alone. Oh, I was glad for her. How could I be anything but glad? I loved her, I cared about her well-being. She was only half alive on this earth, and then she was fully alive with God. So, my grief wasn't for her—her life had been full. My grief was for myself. And if we're honest, we'll admit that this is frequently true. I don't think Jesus wept at the death of Lazarus because He was concerned about Lazarus. In fact, I know He didn't. If anyone ever walked the face of the earth *certain* of the ongoing life after physical death, it was Jesus Christ. His weeping was for Himself. Natural, human grief at the personal loss of a dear friend.

I have used a memorable line from God's great young saint, who left this earth when he was only forty-one, as the theme for this book. Oswald Chambers' writings have all been memorable to me. And although I don't quote often from other authors in my books—mainly because when I read I don't particularly like running onto long quotes—I am using an entire page here from Chambers' classic, *My Utmost For His Highest*. (Don't do as I often do—skip the quote. Read it. Read it more than once, and then think about it a long time. I've done that just today again.)

Receiving One's Self in the Fires of Sorrow

"What shall I say? Father, save me from this hour? But for this cause came I unto this hour. Father, glorify Thy name." John 12:27-29

My attitude as a saint to sorrow and difficulty is not to ask that they may be prevented, but to ask that I may preserve the self God created me to be through every fire of sorrow. Our Lord received Himself in the fire of sorrow, He was saved not *from* the hour, but *out* of the hour.

We say that there ought to be no sorrow, but there *is* sorrow, and we have to receive ourselves in its fires. If we try and evade sorrow, refuse to lay our account with it, we are foolish. Sorrow is one of the biggest facts in life; it is no use saying sorrow ought not to be. Sin and sorrow and suffering *are*, and it is not for us to say that God has made a mistake in allowing them.

Sorrow burns up a great amount of shallowness, but it does not always make a man better. Suffering either gives me my self or it destroys my self. You cannot receive your self in success, you lose your head; you cannot receive your self in monotony, you grouse. The way to find your self is in the fires of sorrow. Why it should be so is another matter, but that it is so is true in the Scriptures and in human experience. You always know the man who has been through the fires of sorrow and has received himself, you are certain you can go to him in trouble and find that he has ample leisure for you. If a man has not been through the fires of sorrow, he is apt to be contemptuous, he has no time for you. If you receive your self in the fires of sorrow, God will make you nourishment for other people.

If you are burning in the fires of a recent sorrow, I can

hear you say—or at least think—"Who wants to be nourishment for other people? I want my loved one back!" Or, "I want my loved one well again and strong as he or she used to be—not this flabby, helpless wrack of bones lying in a bed unable to do a single thing to help me."

Don't castigate yourself if that was your first reaction. It is a very human reaction. But we can pick it up from there and see God in it. Can see that Jesus did not tell us that we were to learn to ignore ourselves or beat ourselves to extinction. He told us that we were to *find* ourselves by *losing*. By laying down. As we are attempting to make clear in this book—by leaving ourselves alone in His hands.

He also said we were to love ourselves. "Thou shalt love thy neighbor *as thyself*." God does not disapprove of self-love. He only disapproves of self-pampering. Of self-pity. And it is extremely important that we remember that God never merely disapproves of anything for the sake of disapproving. Whatever He urges us to do or not to do is urged upon us *only* because, as our Creator, He and He alone knows what works for us and what works against us. He came that we might, in His own words, have a more abundant life. Not a squeezed-in, stifled life of dos and don'ts.

In many ways, we're living in a frightening age. I feel it at times like a heavy cloak thrown over my head cutting off truly fresh air. And yet, the very permissiveness of our times is being *used* by the all-redemptive God who, if we give Him half a chance, wastes nothing. There isn't a human being alive who has yet dared believe how thoroughly God will use anything that happens to His loved ones. When I first wrote my book *No Pat Answers* dealing with the facts of sorrow and tragedy, many persons just weren't interested in the subject. Many hesitated to give the book as a gift because it might be "morbid." In the few years since its publication, there has come a deluge of widely read books on death, sorrow, illness—incurable illnesses—often written by the dying persons themselves. Such books—of inestimable value—are now "permitted" by us, the readers. These books are selling now because we, the readers, have gotten more rightly permissive with ourselves. We're permitting ourselves to face the facts of life. And illness and death are both integral parts of life. Whatever the reason for this new interest in facing facts as they are, God is using it all to "burn up a great amount of shallowness" in us as thinkers. Here is Oswald Chambers again: "Sorrow burns up a great amount of shallowness, but it does not always make a man (or a woman) better. Suffering either gives me my self or it destroys my self."

Do we allow circumstances to "give" us our selves when we leave ourselves alone in those circumstances? Yes. This is something of what Jesus meant when He admonished us to lose our lives in order to find them. So, we can choose. We can destroy our selves in deep wells of self-pity or we can find our selves by losing—by *losing* our defensive selves to God.

I have wished often for a chance to sit down with Oswald Chambers and talk out this problem of human suffering. Some readers have thought Chambers hard, unrelenting. Too tough. I don't see this. Even as a young man, he saw deeply into the heart of both God and man. He was a realist all the way. "We say that there ought to be no sorrow, but there *is* sorrow. . . . If we try and evade sorrow, refuse to lay our account with it, we are foolish." Hard? No. Kind. Dishonesty is never kind. Honesty, in the final analysis, is. Chambers is simply being honest. Realistic. Life is *not* fair. There is sorrow. There has always been sorrow. He lived his brief forty-one years in a close, personal relationship with the God of love. The God who *is* love. He sacrificed a longed-for career as an artist in order to be a friend to that God who is love. In one sense, whether he knew it or not, Oswald Chambers was a young man in a hurry. In such a few years, he saw more deeply into life's dilemmas than most of us ever see. He saw beyond the temporary shatterings. Faithfully, his wife took shorthand notes on his brief lectures during his lifetime. I can almost see him pouring out his discoveries, one after another, while there was still time. Discoveries which require a lifetime for most of us. His writings served me well as a beginning Christian. They still serve me. He knew me. He knew you. "You cannot receive (find) your self in success, you lose your head." True. "You cannot receive (find) your self in monotony, you grouse." Also true.

But sorrow—deep, searing sorrow of whatever nature—destroys not us, if we are open to God, but the "shallowness." And losing our heads in success or grousing in monotony is surely shallow behavior. Receiving ourselves—finding ourselves—in the fires of sorrow, Chambers contends, is the way to kindness. I believe that when we give kindness, we find it. And kindness heals. Grousing about the monotonous aspects of life, boasting in success, do not make us kind. They shut us off in tight, compartmentalized boxes of "pampered self." But sorrow—*if* we have received ourselves in it, if we have permitted God even to *begin* to make use of it—melts away our "contemptuousness." We become available. Tender. Open. Vulnerable. Is there a more vulnerable sight in all human history than Christ hanging on His cross and blessing those who put Him there?

One of the fires of sorrow through which many must pass is that of living through days of extreme illness in the family. There is work to do. Monotonous, backbreaking hard work at times. Perhaps all the time. The days run together in a kind of boundaryless haze, and we wonder if anything will ever change. I spoke yesterday on the telephone with one of my dearest and most saintly friends in Chicago. Her mother, after a third fall, is undoubtedly bedfast for life. My friend has given her own life to both her parents. Unselfishly—foolishly, some of us have thought at times—but freely and with God's love. She has done this for her entire lifetime, and she is no longer young.

"It will end," I said. "I am going to pray that your mother is set free soon to go home."

"Yes," she answered. "And I no longer feel guilty about that prayer. The poor darling is so wretched this way."

There was a silence on the wire, and then I said, "She'll be fine then."

My friend said, "I've tried to take care of them both, but no one can do that the way Jesus can."

There wasn't a tiny hint of self-pity in her voice. There has never been in all the years of her own self-giving. And then, for the remainder of our conversation, she said such encouraging things to me about my work, gave such spirit-lifting insights, that all I could think of was the line from Chambers: "If you receive yourself in the fires of sorrow, God will make you nourishment for other people." She nourished me.

Some of what you read in this book came to me from another friend, Ellen Urquhart, who led me to Christ so long ago. She has learned, is still learning, to receive herself in the fires of her own sorrow. Sorrow born of her late husband's long, long illness and then his death. And now her own almost unbroken solitude and illness. And yet she has spent hours praying, thinking, reading—then sending on her conclusions to me for use in this book. I am more than grateful and, because of her, believe more than ever now that "If you receive yourself in the fires of sorrow, God will make you a nourishment for other people."

Some time ago at an autographing party for my novel, *Maria,* the upbeat mood was shattered when a young woman approached the table where I was signing books.

"I know I'm out of place here," she snapped, her young face hard and deeply lined. "I know you're in no frame of mind to hear a question like this. I've read a lot of your nonfiction, so-called religious books. I read *Maria.* I just don't believe any of it is true. Maria could not have found peace so surely after the death of her husband. What you write is just not true! Life just isn't that way." Tears began to stream down her face, but she held her voice firm. "I lost my husband not long ago, and I'm bitter. I expect to stay that way."

I didn't say anything for a moment, then I asked, "How long ago?"

"Six months today."

"You haven't given yourself much time, have you?"
She shrugged.

"Do you know Jesus Christ in a personal way? Do you believe that His heart is broken for you too?"

She laughed. "No."

And that was her dilemma.

All of what is said here, all of what Oswald Chambers wrote, all of what Jesus Christ said during His life on earth is predicated on the fact of God's grace operative in the believer. Oh, of course, there are strong human beings who manage to recover—outwardly, anyway, when sorrow strikes—without a conscious knowledge of Christ. Hard work helps—even with God's grace. Time helps—even with God's grace. But to *find* one's self in the fires of sorrow is far more than a mere recovery so that daily life can go on.

Finding oneself—the tough, necessary act of finding one's real self—in the midst of sorrow must follow the transaction of business on the grounds of the redemption. And then, by God's ever-present, ever-flowing grace, one must leave oneself resolutely alone.

The temptation to cry out "Poor me!" "Why me?" will come again and again. It may never stop coming. But for nearly thirty years I have believed and tried to live by the fact that Jesus not only came to earth for me, not only died for me, but on that very cross asked my "Why?" for me.

He finished it all right there at Golgotha. He finished it all—for everyone. And in His finished work is the beginning of new life (daily new life) even in the fires of sorrow. No writer, no speaker can explain this.

Jesus Himself is the explanation.

Leave Your Self Alone *in Change*

I'VE SAT FOR a long time before beginning the writing of this chapter. I've smiled to myself a few times, thinking, "One could write half a book, a whole book on the subject!" A frown follows the smile. Some recent changes depress me—until I remember that change, too, is covered for us *if* we learn even a little about leaving ourselves alone in it.

How is it covered? How do even those of us who follow Jesus Christ learn to feel at home in these times of seemingly sudden, certain complex change? How do those of us who have lived as adults through the thirties, forties, fifties, sixties, and seventies cope with the starkly differing characteristics of each decade just past? Isn't it normal to expect basics, at least, to remain firm? Isn't it normal to expect that what we feel we've learned about living will go on applying? What of the sincere, well-meaning grandmothers who write to me in abject despair over the "permissive" behavior of their beloved grand-children? "What's happened to—everything?" one woman wrote. How, in fact, do we handle our inner resentments when a once-full box of cereal from the grocer's shelf turns out these days to be half-empty—a new notation on the package informing us that the contents may "shake down" in transportation. True, we can join and support consumer's groups, but their good results are slow and some of us have only so long to live.

How do we cope without anger and self-pity when the developers go on building one unneeded shopping center after another, cutting down great trees which have shaded and rested us for years, and paving over acres of ground so that there is no way for a heavy rainstorm not to bring problems? Of course, we can attend "public hearings" and commissioners' meetings, and we can and must speak our minds. I've spent months doing this in the past ten years on the island where I live. But the development goes wildly on, the great trees continue to fall, the once porous, absorbent, sandy earth is covered with more and more concrete.

When I first found St. Simons Island, there were less than three thousand people here. Now the population has climbed to nearly twelve thousand. I would be glad if everyone on earth could live here, I love it so. But even now, for those of us who knew it "then," it is in many ways no longer St. Simons Island. The quality of life is changing so fast that I notice a difference every time I drive down Frederica Road to the grocery store. The cherished wilderness is no more. How do I contain what on some days approaches bitterness over the loss? Joyce and I have worked hard to build the home we have here. This island seemed, when we found it in 1961, to be exactly the place we'd searched for for so long. Now look! Our fears and anxieties over the quality of life run deep, deep as we drive the once sun-streaked, tree-shaded main road. I curb myself on those trips now. And I can feel Joyce struggling to control herself too. We try just to ride along, keeping our minds elsewhere. There is no way we can forget those "old days" when our happy talk was mainly repeated exclamations of "Look at that Island light in those trees! Look at the violets along the roadside this year—they're even thicker than last year!" Now we try, and almost always fail, to keep silent about the naked stump of the huge oak we always loved and watched for, the cropped-off, widened, maimed roadsides where once the wildflowers grew in such dizzying profusion.

What's the answer here? There, where you live? What is one person to do? You may live in an urban area where taking a walk at night—or even in daylight—is taboo. I well remember in my young days in Chicago, when I'd partied or written late into the night, that I thought nothing of walking my dog at two in the morning in the alleyway behind my apartment. I thought nothing of it and nothing happened. Am I living too much in the past? What do I do with those memories?

What do you do, if you were young and eager for change in the sixties? Have you given up? Has the change been so different from what you meant it to be that you feel lost, rudderless now? Or have you settled in and decided to get what's yours as everyone else seems to be doing? If you're in your thirties now, have you coped with the fact that young people no longer risk their necks to try to change society?

I am moving into the age when I'm beginning to understand some of the fears and complexities and seemingly unsolvable problems of growing old. I have to take a good ten to fifteen minutes of vigorous exercise every morning in order to get the kinks out of my muscles when I wake up. I mentioned this to a doctor friend, and he only laughed. "Oh, that's just a touch of rheumatism." Rheumatism? A word connected only with the elderly in my mind for all these years! Me—rheumatism? Why, my grandmother always had that. And she was *old*. And then I begin to count back and realize that when she had it so painfully, she was only in her late fifties! Some of you who read this are in your late seventies and eighties, even in your nineties. And, from your lofty pinnacles, you will consider me young at sixty-three. Certainly, I do not consider myself old most of the time—and the secret lies there. The less I *consider* myself at all, the better off I am.

How do we cope with the change in our economic situations? Remember the day when a roll of five hundred first-class stamps cost fifteen dollars? Fifteen dollars! Now when I place an order for a roll of five hundred first-class stamps, I must write a check in the amount of seventy-five dollars! Next year maybe more. I don't recall feeling too resentful of this until a first-class letter sent to my friend, Clara Marie Gould, just across the marshes and salt creeks in Brunswick, Georgia, arrived one month later. That day, I really resented the seventy-five-dollar check. My electric bill is now two and a half times what it cost to heat and cool the same house five years ago. And on and on. I'm sure that some of you don't feel sorry for me at all, and truthfully, I don't want you to. I know that in some parts of the country light bills are far higher than mine.

Grocery bills are, of course, out of sight, and the farmers who grow the food we pay for are, ironically, having it tough. Economics are as far out of my scope of comprehension as are space shots, except for my own bank balance which is shrinking as my income purchases less and less. I'm far from hungry, but laying away that certain amount against the day when I can no longer sit for long hours at this typewriter gets more difficult with the passing of every year. The people who are truly in a place of suffering from economic changes are those who have to put things back on the grocery shelves because there isn't enough money to pay for them at the checkout counter.

"I'm learning a lot about God these days," an elderly lady who lives alone wrote not long ago. "I'm thankful I can still hobble to the store by myself and thankful that I have always liked macaroni and rice. They are good stretchers. I can make a half pound of meat last for nearly a week with these blessed stretchers. The folks I feel sorry for are the women with big families to feed. I only have to worry about feeding one old lady."

The secret again: She who, by most standards, deserves pity is not considering herself much at all. She's thinking about the women who have to stretch the grocery budget to feed a hungry family. Well, true enough, you say. But what a meager way to live.

It is meager and depressing, and it is hard.

And I don't think we'll get far at all by comparing one person's plight with another's. What we *must* do is count our blessings. I managed to get started today by doing it. I'm tired. I haven't been as well as usual after a bout with an obscure virus a few weeks ago. I just plain woke up in (for me) a rare mood of depression and weariness. But before I had counted very many blessings, my mood lifted. And by the time I finished exercising and had the old muscles limbered up a little, I was exclaiming over the buds on the tall trees outside my office window. But there have been days when none of that worked at all. And those days I well know have to do mainly with change. Swift change. Swift and baffling.

The changes in your life may not be exactly like mine, but the clue to handling all change is the same. One of the big changes for me lies in the fact that it is just not as much fun as it once was to publish books. This does not mean I'm getting blasé about the process. It does not mean that the people at the publishing house are not dear, good, well-meaning, hard-working people. It does have to do with bigness and growth. They're all too busy to have as much fun as we used to have. Publishing, as with everything else, gets more complex. Because of the computer age, less personal. I know these things. I accept them. But on the days when I feel depressed, I think back to the "old days" when there was genuine, fulfilling excitement—fun—in the bringing out of a new book. (Thank heaven, I still find this fulfilling enthusiasm among my readers!)

When I consider myself *in change*, I can become filled with self-concern and old-fashioned self-pity.

Well, I'm not alone in my self-considerations. My mail indicates that you're worried too about the quality of life, about future security, about your health, about the destruction of God's earth, about the general, impersonal bigness of the world around us. Perhaps you live on your Social Security check alone. Thank heaven for Social

Security, but it too has grown to such gigantic proportions that it seems often in danger of toppling.

And yet . . . and yet.

If you haven't recently read the last two verses of the eighth chapter of Romans, here they are:

For I am convinced that neither death nor life, neither angels nor demons, neither the present nor the future, nor any powers, neither height nor depth, nor anything else in all creation, will be able to separate us from the love of God that is in Christ Jesus our Lord.

And He, Jesus Christ, *is* "the same yesterday, today, and forever."

Some of you undoubtedly are saying (particularly if this is a bad day for you), "Oh, I knew she'd say something like that!"

What else is there to say? Turn it around and think what things would be like if we could not know for a fact that Jesus Christ will not change. *Cannot* change. By His very nature, He is both the beginning and the end. And all that lies between. And that is all there is.

I awoke today not wanting to write. Feeling I had little or nothing to say. But I did turn to Him, and I thought something like this: "I'm flat. I'm empty. I need You." I had not even meant to write a chapter on leaving ourselves alone in change. By the time my morning exercises were finished, the idea had come. He heard me, and He already knew so well what was bugging me today that I didn't need a long string of pleading words when I turned to Him. What I did need to do was to *leave myself alone* in the way I felt when I first woke up. I did not feel any great surge of vital faith. This is never needed. What is needed is to *know*—regardless of how we feel or of what is happening—at least something of what this God we follow is really like.

That has been a theme running like a river through my books. It will always be because on this fact rests the solace of all of human life. *God is knowable.* He came to earth for that reason. He is always attentive, waiting only for us to turn to Him in our need. He, of all persons, knows the negative effect of change on a human being. After all, He was lauded as a king, had flowers spread before Him as He rode triumphantly into Jerusalem just one week before they turned on Him to murder Him. His closest friends fled, ran for their own lives. Considered only themselves. He seems to have considered Himself only twice—once, in the Garden of Gethsemane, when He asked the Father if it were possible that He, Jesus, could be spared the change He knew lay ahead. Then on the cross, He asked the Father why He had apparently deserted Him in His hour of darkest need. This Jesus Christ, who knows from experience what it means to be human, to fear change, to dread the future, will always be the first to understand our fears and dreads. But in both His moments of self-consideration, *in His heart* He was willing, if it turned out to be the Father's will, to endure the change.

We falter when we over-consider ourselves while expecting the Father to get us out of our jams, to make life easier, to bring back the "good old days." What He is saying is that He needs us to be His friends in the midst of whatever is going on.

My telephone rang about half-way through the preceding page. "What are you writing about?" I was asked. I told my friend that I was trying to write a book about some of the freedom I'd found when I managed to leave myself alone in the tight places. "Oh," he said, "but aren't there times when we have to think about ourselves first?" I thought a minute and then said, "Well, I think our ideas on that subject have to do with how much we know about God Himself. There's no other way I can see to find out what real love is all about because God is love *in person*. And love always *considers the loved one first.* Perhaps," I added, "it's a matter of semantics."

In a way it is. I believe that indeed at times we *must* make a case for ourselves. And yet, in doing so, we desperately need to count on the wisdom that comes from God and not upon even our own best human wisdom. Stating an intelligent case for ourselves is not necessarily self-defense, if we state that case in the Spirit of the One who never, never defended Himself—even against change.

And the change *He* faced meant the difference between life and death.

You know there is a life-changing distance between acting in obedience to the Lord who is our personal friend—whom we know—and in having *religious feelings* that prompt us to say or to think, "Oh, I'd better trust God in this." We *can't* trust the God we don't know personally. But once we get into the business of learning about His true nature, trust is automatic. I do not trust Him simply because I feel it's the moral or wise thing to do. I trust Him because I've learned enough about what He's like to know that only He is totally trustworthy.

And only He does not change.

In one way, we can give thanks for the changes which shock and offend and scare us, leaving us anxious and confused. Perhaps Paul meant something like this when he wrote that we were to give thanks *in everything.* If once-beautiful, shadow-slashed, tree-sheltered Frederica Road were still as it used to be, I'd be thinking only of the beauty as I ride along it now. The ugliness of the change forces me to think on the God I follow, who will never, can never be anything but the God He showed us in Jesus Christ. When I was young and didn't know the meaning of stiff muscles in the mornings or weariness along the way, I had no need to call on Him for strength. I had enough of my own. I had known no grief, and so I needed no solace.

Where my books are concerned, I was enjoying it all too much back in the warmer, more personalized world of publishing really to get down to thinking about my reason for writing them in the first place. But now that publishing has changed, I am cornered, and the corner can be bright, because for much of the way I now see that my joy in writing and publishing has come from Him.

Joy is God in the marrow of our bones. And His joy never changes.

Leave Your Self Alone *in Your Judgments*

Is this possible?

Indeed, how *can* we leave ourselves alone when it is the self that makes the judgments?

We can't—on our own. We don't even want to. But when the self is enlightened by the very nature of God, we can make fewer narrow judgments and far more on the side of love. Love? Shouldn't judgments be made from wisdom? From experience—past and present? From learning? From weighing issues pro and con? Yes. All of these enter in, and yet I am able in most instances to make sharper, clearer judgments (discernments) by using *love* as my guide. Love moves always outward—toward the other person. Toward identification with the other person's point of view and away from the view which we've always held.

Love moves toward the loved one.

But don't I have to make judgments out of my own mind? Yes. Ultimately. And yet there is a boundless (too often untapped) source available to those who follow Jesus Christ. Paul told us that we are to "Let this mind be in you which was in Christ Jesus." Is there anyone whose judgments you'd rather trust than the judgments of Jesus Christ? Didn't Jesus Himself declare that "the Father judgeth no man, but hath committed all judgment unto the Son?"

Those of us who follow Him truly, with our whole hearts, believe that the Father revealed Himself *as He is* in the Son. And didn't Jesus by His actions, by His will, by His words live out the very life of God on this earth? Believers in the deity of Christ *know* (cannot prove, but know) that in the mind of Jesus Christ is to be found perfect judgment. Since the Father leaves all judgment in the hands of the Son, what characterizes the judgment of the Son?

Love.

Not soft, sentimental, permissive stuff as we often think of love, but that which chastens and corrects and strengthens and blesses and makes new. Love that does not run short of patience. Love that does not consider itself first. Love that *leaves itself alone* in favor of the loved one. Never love that pampers in order to make itself *seem* lovable, but love that gives of itself in honesty. A parent who gives a child anything he or she asks is not showing the judgment of Christlike love because that kind of "love" will result in false values and ingratitude. A friend or relative who submits constantly, who "gives in" day in and day out to the selfish whims of someone else, is not truly loving. This kind of passivity simply protects the outside while the inside of both parties is destroyed. Giving in to that person who has never grown past the spoiled-brat stage is usually taking the easy way for ourselves.

"Her husband let her have her own way for as long as he lived on this earth. It was the only means by which he knew to keep peace in the house." The poor man had made a judgment which appeared to some who knew him to be unselfish. I've come to know his widow now that he is gone, and she is busy going here and there in her life, forcing other relatives and friends to give in as she forced her husband to do. It worked for her so long, why stop?

Jesus in His teachings and in His life and in His death proclaimed and then showed that real love does not "give in"—it *gives to*. And in the giving to, it stands firm. He gave love from the cross to those who had nailed Him there, but in no way did He give in to them.

There are endless clues in the Bible to the nature of the love of God in Christ. The love that backed up His judgments all His earthly life. The love that still backs up the very judgments of God. The love that can, if we are willing to allow our own judgments to be patterned by this love, begin to perfect our thinking and our choices, to sharpen our critical faculties, to heighten our discretions.

Let's begin with what appears to be the most difficult biblical clue: "You have heard that it hath been said, Thou shalt love thy neighbor and hate thine enemy. (This is Jesus talking.) But I say unto you, Love your enemies, bless them that curse you, do good to them that hate you, and pray for them which despitefully use you, and persecute you."

Tough words? Really tough. And impossible, as I see it, without the very mind and heart and spirit of Christ at work in us.

Has man ever truly followed this teaching? The admonition isn't practical, you say? Of course not. If practicality had been enough—a path of pragmatism decided upon at some council table—then Jesus would not have needed to die.

On the cross He demonstrated the power of this kind of love. He prayed for forgiveness for His enemies because His judgment of them was so accurate. "Father, forgive them for they *know not what they do.*" With all their learning and their backbreaking load of religious laws, His enemies were still in spiritual darkness. They did not believe that God Himself hung there in this young man from Nazareth. As a consequence, from *their* viewpoint (and He, in His perfect judgment, could see and understand their viewpoint) they were doing God a favor by ridding the world of this impostor who claimed to be the Son of God. Who broke Sabbath laws by healing the afflicted and causing the blind to see. Who "worked" for the healing of humanity on the Sabbath.

Jesus was able to pray for His enemies who cursed, hated, and despitefully used Him because He knew them. He knew who He was too. He had come directly from the Father and had stayed in unbroken communion with Him through every hour of His earthly life. He had no delusions about either Himself or His enemies. Therefore, His judgments could be perfect, based on perfect love.

Now, how does this help us? How can it help us when we are not possessors of the total insight of God? Well,

Paul says that we are to let God's insight *be in us*. He does not say that we are to work and struggle and finally learn to copy or imitate the insight (the mind) of Christ. He specifically uses the words: *"Let this mind be in you."* Meaning that it is true, true, true that God in His wisdom and His love did work out a way through His Spirit to *live His life in us*. When His life comes, His mind comes with it.

How do we make use of this inestimable gift? By receiving it, of course. But what is the value of receiving any gift if we make no use of it? Nothing of what is written here is new. And yet Christians go on by the thousands tucking God's gifts, wrapped in the tissue paper of religious morality, down, down into the corner of a dark drawer—to save. To save for what?

As I've already written, Lorah Plemmons, one of my dearest friends, died at the age of 102. When she was gone, her daughters found literally heaps of past birthday and Christmas gifts, carefully wrapped and tucked away unused. For sure, this beloved old friend did *not* tuck away God's gifts to her. She possessed almost flawless judgment, the very judgment of God where people were concerned. At her advanced age, no young person shocked or dismayed her. She saw them *where they were*: too young, too inexperienced, too lacking yet in wisdom to be other than what they were. She saw adults who behaved in similar fashion too. She did not waver on her own heaven-bound course, but she was pure, made pure by the forgiveness of Christ. Purity is tough. Durable. Eternal. Innocence is weak, easily disillusioned, transitory. My old friend was not innocent—she was *pure*, and she was wise with the wisdom of God in her daily life. But she did stash away those endless boxes of soap and handkerchiefs and bath powder and aprons.

If it is possible (and we have God's word for it that it is) for us to live out our days *letting* the mind of Christ be in us, then there's hope that we can learn—not to follow only our own thinking, our own experiences, our own prejudices and preferences, but to think and to make judgments that at least show resemblance to His.

And does He ask us to perceive people and events from His point of view just to be arbitrary? Just to be tough on us? Just to prove that all man has written about how difficult the Christian Way is, after all, true? Of course not. The way into the Christian life *is* narrow. There is no room for self-will, for human morality, for good works. There is only room for the open and repentant heart at the first turning *into* the Way. Then, oh, then the Way widens. And it widens because everything God tells us to do is for our good. Many persons flinch at this. I did. Who wants to be "done good"? Well, God is not a do-gooder. Some of us think being do-gooders is being Christian. It isn't. The person who struggles to be moral on his own is no liberated Christian. The Son has not yet had a chance to make that person free. God does not "do us good." He *is* all good, and His mind can be in us *if* we let it—for our good.

In two hard areas in my life, I proved this to be true. I cannot write about them for the protection of other persons, but in two difficult predicaments in my life, when for once I had done nothing wrong— I was being not only used, but somewhat persecuted by two batches of "enemies"—I decided to try out what Jesus commanded. I *left myself alone*, stopped considering me, stopped running from one friend to another telling my precious tale of mistreatment in order to get sympathy, and became willing to learn how to pray for and to love those enemies.

And do you know, it worked.

It not only worked, but at one point—perhaps it was the exact point where I managed to leave me completely alone in the whole thing—loving them and praying for them stopped being difficult.

Of course, the people who use us are not always strangers, or even enemies as such. Children use their parents. Parents use their children. Friends use friends. One of the most subtle temptations for any of us, I believe, is to use a friend without letting the friend catch on that he or she is being used. By masking our actions in seeming kindness. One otherwise good and unselfish man could not cope with a visiting mother-in-law. He "used" another friend by inviting him over every day for the entire time the mother-in-law was around making trouble. You see, when the "outsider" was there, the troublesome relative behaved, stopped nagging, stopped putting my friend down.

About half the time, in fairness to us all, we "use" people without realizing that's what we're doing.

We are not to "use" anyone. We are to love those difficult folk, and we are to pray for them and help them to see themselves through our acts of love.

And we are to do this *through* the power of the mind of Christ which is in us. Once we've really done it, we're apt to smile a little even through our persecution. Why? Because God is not arbitrary. Whatever He tells us to do (and then empowers us to do) works. Makes life less stressful, easier to cope with, more possible to handle.

True, what we are commanded to do is, where our *average* judgments are concerned, against human nature. But human nature was flawed shortly after God created it in His image. He's simply putting forth every effort to bring us back again to the grace and beauty of being the kind of people He intended in the beginning.

Every hard thing God asks of us is an arrow pointing us back to the loveliness of the Garden.

I am not to judge my enemies. I am to let the mind of Christ in me do the judging. Only He knows what hurts us, what twists our viewpoints. Only He knows what hurts and twists the viewpoint of our enemies, of those who despitefully use and persecute us.

And only He can handle us both.

Now, how does all this affect us in other judgments which life requires of us? How, indeed, does leaving ourselves alone and letting the mind of Christ judge through us affect our social consciences? Truthfully, most of us put on the brakes here. Most Christians espouse political and social viewpoints strictly from the place in which they themselves stand in the social scale. Blacks will support the candidate who promises to do the most for them. Labor follows suit. Big business follows suit. As do taxpayers.

Let's get down to a basic—taxes. Do you disapprove of all welfare programs because they increase your own income tax? I'm not discussing all that's so obviously wrong and inefficient and cumbersome and unfair about our current welfare system. We're considering the basics here. Do you feel because you've made it, are a bill-paying, tax-paying, responsible citizen that the devil can take those who haven't made it? Here again, we are not drawing conclusions about who has been victimized by life and who is just plain lazy. Basics.

Do you resent such a large portion of your tax dollar going to help the needy? Have you convinced yourself that anyone who really wants to work can work? Is there to be no allowance for those who are just plain misfits? The truly poor and underprivileged? Does the word "disadvantaged" raise a red flag in your mind?

Well, what did Jesus say in this area?

"Give to him that asketh thee and from him that would borrow of thee, turn not away."

He also told us to give away our coats. Did He mean all this? He did. There is a strong, underlying principle in these startling, even shocking statements which deals with the very nature of the mind of Christ. Of course, He didn't mean for us to give away all our clothing so that we have to go around in the nude. Jesus seldom spoke in externals. There was always a deeper meaning. And that meaning invariably had to do with *judgment*. The quality of the kind of judgments He has a right to expect of us.

And this caliber of judgment has to do directly with His having said to us that whatever we do for the very least person—the most unimportant, unattractive troublesome person—we do directly *for Him*.

You see, what is so hard for us to understand is that He loves all the people who turn us off as much as He loves us.

What of our judgments (good and faulty) where our work is concerned? Our daily lives? The very planning of a day can be traumatic in these times. To carry out these plans can be chaotic, exhausting. Do we use "poor judgment" in expecting too much of ourselves in a single day? Or do we use equally "poor judgment" in planning for our own pleasure? There are wonderful people whose days are scheduled around the golf course. Or the tennis courts almost every day. Wrong? No. But from my narrow viewpoint, I wonder how there can be time enough after family duties are carried out, left for God, for reading, for visiting the sick, etc., if a big block of hours in every day has been spent only in recreation?

In fact, I err on the other side in my judgment. I loathe physical exercise and use poor judgment in getting precious little of the stuff. (It shows too.) When I'm not writing a book, I'm reading a book. There is nothing wrong about either playing tennis or reading a book. Both are important, both worthwhile in their separate ways. But the words of Jesus ring again in the judgment we use in planning both our work and our play: "Inasmuch as ye have done it unto one of the least of these . . . ye have done it unto me." Time spent giving of ourselves to someone in need is time spent worshiping God.

When it comes down to it, my judgment is often poor here. I'd rather read a book than visit the nursing home or write a letter to a lonely person.

Most of us who work for a living have dire need of the very judgment of God in planning ahead. Especially those in executive positions where there is a certain amount of freedom in scheduling the hours of a day. Most especially in work like mine where no one but God prompts me. I can report some progress here. For most of my Christian life I have overworked. A workaholic, as we say with ridiculous pride. There is still a wide stripe of Puritan in some of us. I had no discipline where my writing (my work) was concerned before I met Christ. After I met Him I naturally, as a new Christian, went overboard in trying to compensate. True, I'm more contented when I'm in the midst of a writing project, but after reading biographies of other writers, I learned that few stayed at it as long as I did. The mind of Christ was forming in me, and I began to see myself as feeling quite egotistical that I was such a hard worker. I am now learning (slow progress after all those years) to legislate—to make the judgment to set aside—reading time, playing time every day. One of my problems is that I don't enjoy any form of relaxation other than stimulating conversation, really listening to music (I loathe background music with chit-chat going), and reading books. Nothing wrong with any of my three favorite things to do—except there is no physical exercise involved whatever in any of them. So, I'm forcing—and it is a matter of forcing—myself to take a nap and at least two good, vigorous sets of calisthenics each day. Not enough, perhaps, but for me it's progress.

Many of our human judgments concerning work are based on our need (or desire) to escape. There is nothing wrong with a certain amount of escape. But too much escape into work, into endless parking before a TV screen, into novels—golf, tennis, anything—good though it may be, throws us off balance.

Balance.

Balance is the end result of letting the mind and the judgment of Christ be in us.

"I sit in front of the television all day" a young woman wrote, "and then I have to rush madly around in the late afternoon, making beds, washing breakfast and lunch dishes, at least look busy at preparing dinner when my husband comes home from work."

Escape. Lack of balance. Creating for herself a chaotic, dreadful end of every day.

"Let this mind be in you that was in Christ Jesus."

No matter how much you hate housework and love watching TV, you can leave yourself alone in the planning of one day and try it. No matter how much I loathe physical exercise, I can make myself take a brisk walk or at least add one more set of calisthenics. After I do that, I'll enjoy the book I'm reading even more. My conscience will be free.

And my judgment will have improved.

Leave Your Self Alone *to Grow*

NO ONE CAN ever know us as God knows us. No one else could bear such knowledge—good and bad. But we owe it to ourselves and to God to know as much about our own motives as we possibly can. And yet, if we take this advice and begin a ruthless, extended, headlong, self-examination, we're sunk. We're sunk mainly because whatever we continue to do for a period of time becomes a habit, and the first thing we know *we* have our own full attention to the exclusion of everyone else, including God. I grant that we are urged to do this in book after book of religious writing and even more in the popular best sellers recommending confrontation of one kind or another with our "inner selves." Here again, we are desperately in need of balance. Balance to know ourselves and yet leave ourselves alone enough to grow. There is no greater scourge in all human society than the self-decieved person, some of whom will kill or resort to other violence believing themselves called to behave so. There is also the troublesome scourge of the man or woman who feels himself or herself to be so interesting that the rest of us must bow down night and day. Lack of self-knowledge is not a virtue.

You see, the Bible plainly tells us that "the heart is deceitful above all things. . . . Who can understand it?" In other words, who can know our hearts *fully* but God? It is true that seeing helps. A competent psychiatrist can help us see our needs, our shortcomings, our various complexes. But after we see them, what then?

What do we do with our guilt?

And in so many areas of human life, Jesus Himself, who came to earth not only to show us the Father's heart, but to explain human life as well, tells us plainly that we are also to *learn all we can learn about Him*, the Son of God. "Learn of me," He urged, "and ye shall find rest unto your souls. For my yoke is easy, and my burden is light."

For me, at least, the way is cleared by these words of Jesus. *If* at the same time in which I am open to learn more about myself, to assess my faults and weaknesses more directly, to recognize my good points, I simultaneously open myself to learn of Him, the *creative interaction begins*. I may be shocked a little or a lot every day by what I learn of myself, but the shock is cushioned by new knowledge of the One who created and then redeemed me.

In fact, if I give my attention to learning more and still more about the One who trusted me enough to condone a creative kind of self-love—and He did: "Love your neighbor *as* yourself"—I can fully expect to progress not only toward self-acceptance, but toward true self-respect.

Again, what did Oswald Chambers mean when he wrote: "Transact business on the grounds of the Redemption and then leave yourself resolutely alone"? Again, what do I mean by writing a book titled *Leave Yourself Alone*? Just this: If we brush aside all the breast-beating and self-analysis and mental and emotional flagellation about which both secular and religious writers have written for so long, if we "transact business" on the ground of the *erasing*, the *blotting out* forgiveness of God in Jesus Christ, we can begin to see something of what Jesus meant when He said that His yoke is easy and His burden light. No matter what we find in the depths of our inner beings, there is something that can and will be done about it. There is no learning of Jesus Christ without learning of His power and eagerness to forgive, to blot out. Redemption is at the center of the very nature of the Father Himself, and "He (Jesus Christ) hath revealed Him."

"Come to me, all you who are weary and burdened, and I will give you rest."

Have you ever noticed that in this familiar and much-quoted passage from Matthew's Gospel, Jesus does not even mention all the rot and error and sin in us? He mentions only sin's consequences: weariness and a burden on our backs. It is the human overemphasis on the ugliness of the human condition which has repelled so many through the years. The reality is that we are seldom as aware of our sin as of our exhaustion from it.

Now, before anyone despairs of my theology, read this: The human condition is ugly in its helplessness, it's sin, it's willful selfishness without the redeeming touch of God. One only has to listen to a single five-minute news broadcast to know this. As I write today, fresh terrorism and the expected bloody retaliation are again in the news from the Middle East. A prominent Italian statesman has been kidnapped, and all five of his bodyguards were left dead in the street. Just a few days ago a young woman, the mother of five children—a woman loved and admired by everyone who knew her—was shot in the head while on her job at the desk of a local motel. Within twenty minutes after she was murdered, a man in the same position at another motel a few miles away was shot in the same manner. Enough of the news. This is human nature in operation without the redemptive touch of the One who died with His arms stretched out toward the whole sinful world.

But Jesus Christ was (is) a realist. He knew the human condition well enough to know that, left on our own, our yokes are heavy and our burdens are crushing. Those of us who have tried valiantly to live our adult lives without a sense of Christ's touch, without His redemption's freeing power, do not need to be told that we're in trouble. Especially those nonconformists among us. It is harder, I suppose, for the moral conformists—the sheltered, unexposed, self-righteous—among us to see our need. But sooner or later life deals us a staggering blow, and we find out about that heavy burden.

Jesus knows us utterly. In the face of our own self-deception, even in the midst of what seems to us a sincere statement—"I didn't mean to make it come out that way, God"—He still knows the times when we really *did mean* it to come out that way. He knows.

Jesus knows, and isn't that a relief?

Jesus Christ also knows Himself. In case you're wondering what that has to do with our knowing ourselves or leaving ourselves alone to let Him work His will in our lives, consider this: He said, "Come unto *me*." He did not say, "Come unto the organized church" (although He is there). He did not say, "Come unto the Bible" (although He is there too). He did not say, "Look at how helplessly sinful and evil you are. You are surely going to come to a ghastly end on your own." *He was a realist.* About us and about Himself. Those who have been frightened or shamed into some religious experience may not necessarily have found God *as He is*. Although when possible, He will lay His hand on the human heart even in the face of scare psychology.

But Jesus Christ is the magnet—the only magnet which can truly draw the human heart as the human heart actually is. He knew that because He knew Himself. Knew Himself enough to declare that "I, if I be lifted up . . . will draw *all* men unto me."

The older I become, the more I am convinced that the only way in which I can *bear* to know myself is in the healing, encouraging, forgiving presence of Jesus Christ. But there I can bear it. Where He is, hope is. More than hope—assurance. And He has said that He will never leave us nor forsake us. That He is with us always—to stay. Through anything.

But how can I ever get to know myself, even in the reassuring presence of Jesus Christ, if I leave myself alone? This book will have failed utterly if it is not understood by now that what Chambers meant, what I mean, is that we transact business on the grounds of the redemption *first*, and *then* leave ourselves in the hands of God.

Of course we'll go on being self-concerned, but we'll see a way through it. Of course we'll fall now and then into the mire of self-pity, but we'll know where to reach for that Hand up. Of course we'll be disappointed. Of course we'll fail. Of course we'll let down those expecting our best. But if that business of redemption has been transacted on the sound basis—the ground of His redeeming love—we will at least have access to the truth about how much too much we've complained about what happened to us in our past and what may happen in our future. We will find more freedom from ourselves when we pray, more balance in our work, our conversation— even political and religious. We will understand a little better how to hide our hearts in that redeeming love when there is illness and death or when we face change. Our judgments can and will be altered by this same redeeming love if we have transacted business on it. And if we are, at least in a measure, leaving ourselves alone.

Leaving ourselves alone simply means that after we see clearly that we are in a certain situation and are beginning to have self-centered, protective reactions toward it, we *can* decide, we do have access to the power to decide right then and there whether God Almighty *or* we can do the best job of coping.

Read all the analytical books you like, study all your "passages" and "zones," good and "erroneous," but the time must come for us all, if we are to live adequately in a world which has always been harsh, unfair, and burdensome, when we see and act upon the fact of the presence of the Redeemer, Jesus Christ *in the midst of*. In the midst of joys and intense happiness as well as in the midst of turmoil and grief. Poring only over tomes which point out our already evident failures can be a waste. Poring only over tomes which warn us about the difficult "passages" which may or may not be ahead can be anxiety-building. Valuable in the realm of self-knowledge, but Jesus urged us to *know Him*. At the same time reassuring us, because of who He is, that He knows us and will never lead or even nudge us in a direction that will complicate any future event or increase any fault already present.

Some who have read my books simply refuse to believe (wrongly) that I am ever in a dark, confused passage in my own life. Refuse to believe that I'm dull and blank at times in the presence of Jesus Christ. That I, the same as you, go through times of preoccupation with my work when in the moment just before I fall asleep at night, I think: "I'm not giving You enough time, Lord. I'm living this period of my life for me. I'm trying too hard to solve my own problems. I must do better. I . . . must . . . do . . . better. . . ."

And the next morning I wake up seething to get back into a certain period in history—eager to straighten out a scene which didn't come off the day before—and go on being my own master. My own master. I am *not* doubting God during these times while I'm in charge. I am *not* in rebellion against Him. He continues as an integral part of my life. But *I* am doing much of the guiding. Nothing antagonistic on my part. Just blah. And busy. Even my busyness is usually in His direction, but this is a subtle trap for those of us who have once and for all settled our commitment to Christ. It's even a subtle trap for those of us who have settled it once and for all that He is eternally committed to us. We simply tend not to give Him much direct attention during these times.

After a while, though, I miss Him. And I find myself with the Gospel of John (my favorite) open beside my typewriter. Or I stop what I'm doing and look out the window and *think* about Him. "You're still right here, aren't You?" Yes. He's still right here. And nine times out of ten at the end of one of those times of self-management, I feel burdens drop from my shoulders which hadn't seemed like burdens at all. Subtle. Oh, so subtle are those times of overt self-management.

Times of attending only to my *self*.

Self-propelling my life.

All right, up to a point.

But, definitely not leaving myself alone.

And there is, to my knowledge, no way to leave oneself alone except to remain sensitively cognizant of what Leslie Weatherhead called "The Transforming Friendship." Except for Jesus Christ, I'm the most interesting and attractive person I know (to me). Except for Him, I'd rather think about me, or at least allow my thoughts to wing no further afield than my immediate circle of people.

It is particularly in these times when for one reason or another Jesus Christ has been pushed to the margin of my life and I am not leaving myself alone that I begin to wonder what might happen to me in my old age. What will happen, I reason, unless I work still harder now? Nonsense. I work as hard as my limitations allow anyway. And didn't He say He Himself would sustain me "even to old age and gray hairs"? Well, I realize again that I'm already quite gray. So, shouldn't I prepare? Surely, God seems to do nothing about the ghastly conditions in many of our nursing homes. And off I go on another tangent of self-attending under the guise of "concern for society as a whole." There is, after all, a difference between attending to business and attending to ourselves.

Once I'm back in conscious contact with Him I find such self-attention a complete bore. It is also tiring.

Can one leave onself alone in grief? Yes. I've tried it, and it's possible. Well, does it stop the grief? No. But it allows it to run its normal course, *not* kept alive and screaming for constant attention by daily talks with friends about it, by seeking sympathy. This wasn't so difficult for me simply because so few persons could even imagine the depth of my grief at the loss of an editor. A houseman. A 102-year-old neighbor. They were all my dear, treasured friends. I still miss them keenly—every day. But the Healer of all grief is free to sustain me exactly as I leave myself alone *in my grief.* Exactly as I remain sensitive to Him and not to myself. I have learned so much about the nature of Christ through the deaths of these three persons, so important to my daily life, that I doubt my success at ever imparting the whole process to anyone else. We must each learn for ourselves.

Now, we move into an area in which I've had little or no experience. Leaving ourselves alone in our *own* illnesses. Is this the most difficult of all? Perhaps. For most of my life, I have been in good health. Except for an apparently inherited tendency to high blood pressure, I am now in good health. There is no way that I can speak from actual experience here. But then, if I wrote only from my own experience, what I write would be of little value to you. I do not have the burdens or the joys or the confusions or the hours of work—repeated every day—which go along with having children. My pressures are of a different nature. I have, at least at this writing, not had to leave myself alone in the face of serious illness.

I have known those who have had this experience. I have known those who have succeeded beyond my belief, even as I saw it happen. I've saved a letter which I received some time ago for this very spot. It is a letter from a woman, a wife and mother and homemaker, whose faith and peace in Jesus Christ still have me in awe. Her name is Ann, and she lives in a small town in Illinois with her children and her husband, Leonard, who is also my friend. Ann is not old. She couldn't be more than forty, if that. I have, through the years, watched God make miracles for Ann and Leonard. I expect them both to be strong in times of crisis. But this letter raised my spiritual horizon so fast, it almost made me dizzy!

For the first four pages of a fairly long letter, Ann told me in her amusing style about the children, about the stray kitten one of the boys had rescued, about a trip the family planned to visit their seventeen-year-old, Jane, who now lives and works in Colorado.

Here I will pick up Ann's letter as she wrote it:

Also as best we can, Len and I are preparing the children for another trip that soon I'll be making, Genie. A trip home, to be with my Lord. I have had two terminal liver illnesses since 1973. One of them, cirrhosis, has now reached the latter stages.

A wonderful, wonderful Christian couple in Elmhurst has accepted our desire as God's will for them to care for and finish raising our precious children when this time comes. We have signed papers to this effect last week at our attorney's office.

I am satisfied and at rest that my Lord's ways are best and His will is perfect! Whether He will choose for me to be taken home slowly . . . or quickly, by the rush of uncontrolled bleeding, I don't know. But *I do know* that I am willing to accept whichever He thinks best. And that I totally accept His choice to call me home, even though if my will could be His direct will, I'd choose to finish raising our children and go home after Len. I am neither afraid, bitter nor anxious! I am at rest and my soul knows no turmoil.

Life is so full of wonderment and amazement for the Christian! It's only God who can turn dirty dishes, a messed up house and piles of soiled laundry into a mother's heaven! It's only God who can turn a mother's scream of terror at a frog placed deliberately by little fingers in the clothes hamper into a good, freeing laugh. It's only God who can stretch a pay check to cover all our needs. . . . I could go on and on about what only He can do, because to a wife and "mommie" only God is the solution for all matters—for every tiny detail.

The school bus has just zoomed by, so I must close to prepare a snack. You'd swear they hadn't eaten for days when they come in! "Hi, Mom, what's to eat?" This shouted by all three as they toss everything in a heap on the davenport. Immediately, I'm "in their world"—all of us talking at the same time.

How's that for leaving oneself alone?

Ann concluded her letter by telling me that only the necessary few friends knew anything at all about her impending death. "Why burden them?" And then followed a cheery narrative of the "best Christmas" they'd ever had with Ann just home from the hospital.

No comment of mine is necessary here. I wouldn't know what to say anyway. Except that Ann, loving her husband and children as I know she does, could never do this, could never go on living creatively in her condition, without minute-by-minute grace from the Lord she loves with a child-heart. The kind of child-love that enables one to be a great and strong woman in the face of the worst thing that could happen to her and to her little family.

Grace.

My own head is whirling as I write this. I feel almost ill myself from identification with Ann and Len. And yet, because they are the ones facing what they face—and not I—they are, this minute, the steady recipients of the grace that can make sense out of nonsense. Can bring joy out of grief. Can bring strength out of weakness, peace out of rebellion.

Now and then a reader will write to me: "I wish you wouldn't tell about such dreadful happenings. I just know I could never face anything like that—even as a Christian."

Not a surprising comment. That person had no need at that moment for that downpouring of grace. It has been said and said and I must repeat again: He never sends grace until the moment of our need. If He did, we would, being human, begin to depend on that store of grace instead of the One who Himself is "full of grace and truth."

If someone has just hurt you or broken your heart, if someone you love has just died, if you have just been told that you have six months to live on earth—all the grace you need is there, waiting for you to receive it.

As long as we are pulled inward, wringing our own hands in despair and self-attention, we don't have a free hand to reach for God's grace. If we mean to leave ourselves alone, we must, we *must* keep a hand free to reach for what He has to give. He will know, invariably, exactly what it is we need.

Those "dreadful happenings" don't occur as often as the daily hang-ups, the annoyances that pass. But there is no way for us to be prepared for the big ones unless we have already begun to learn the art of leaving ourselves alone in the daily round of little ones. Complaints, no matter how small, are self-attentive. A person whose nature seems to be all cantankerous is usually a chronic complainer. And seldom does that person truly respect himself or herself. There is a world of difference between self-protection and self-respect.

You and I, as children of God, as living branches growing from the living Vine, can know self-respect. Too much self-attention blocks that because it blocks growth. Even too much digging into the state of our spiritual selves can block us. *What gets our attention gets us.* "Come unto me," Jesus said. If my attention is on Him, I am free. Free to work and rest and grow.

If our full attention is on God, we don't remember to worry about ourselves. Why? Because all who learn of Him—really find out what Jesus Christ is like—will know beyond the shadow of any doubt that close attention to ourselves is just not necessary. Because if we know Him, we know that every minute His attention is fully upon each one of us.

"Transact business on the grounds of the Redemption and then *leave yourself resolutely alone"*—in peace.